THEODOR BOVERI

Theodor Boveri, 1908.

THEODOR BOVERI
Life and Work of a Great Biologist
1862-1915

FRITZ BALTZER
Translated from the German by
Dorothea Rudnick

University of California Press
BERKELEY AND LOS ANGELES 1967

University of California Press
Berkeley and Los Angeles, California
Cambridge University Press
London, England
Copyright © 1967, by
The Regents of the University of California
Library of Congress Catalog Card Number: 67-21996

Translator's Note

When it was suggested, through the international grapevine connecting embryologists in time and space, that I undertake the translation of Professor Baltzer's memoir of Theodor Boveri, it was not possible for me to refuse. The reasons were numerous, but foremost was the strong feeling that the present generation of American cell biologists has too little contact with the biological groundwork on which the exciting modern advances stand, especially with the German work and even more especially with that of Boveri. A translation of this admirable biography-cum-scientific exposition should find many interested readers and should serve to clarify perspectives.

Despite my linguistic deficiencies I was encouraged by Professor Baltzer's willingness to supervise the English version. The final draft was prepared cooperatively at Berne. Some alterations have been made from the German text. In the present version freer use has been made of quotations from the writings of E. B. Wilson, whose masterly evaluations of Boveri's scientific contributions were originally expressed in an English that cannot be bettered; Boveri's letter in comic Bavarian dialect, addressed to Röntgen in 1912 (on pp. 69–70 of the German edition) has been omitted as totally untranslatable; and the final chapter on the Rectoral Address has been revised.

In translating, we have endeavored, in so far as the English language permits, to retain the timbre of the original, especially in the passages where Boveri's own words are heard. We are much indebted to Dr. Salome Waelsch in New York for help with difficulties in the original stages. Warmest thanks are due Dr. Emile Audétat in Biel, Switzerland, who later read and improved the manuscript, and Dr. Margret Boveri, for revision of the biographical section and for the loan of the photograph of the *Seehaus* at Höfen.

The University of California Press has been most helpful and encouraging during the course of this project, and we offer our appreciation to them as well.

DOROTHEA RUDNICK

New Haven, Connecticut

Publisher's Note

In the original German publication, the bibliography was restricted to scientific literature, and this has not been altered. A reader wishing to use the scientific references will find that there are, for his convenience, four separate lists of citations: (1) Boveri's own scientific bibliography; (2) obituary articles on Boveri; (3) all the remaining publications referred to in the text; and (4) all the scientific publications emanating from Boveri's institute in Würzburg during his directorship, with the exception, of course, of his own works.

Items in the first two lists have been numbered in series with arabic numerals (1-67), and reference to any of these publications in the text is made by way of these same numerals, enclosed in parentheses, sometimes with a specific page designated. The items in the third list are not numbered but are arranged alphabetically by author's name; these are referred to in the text by the author's last name and the year of publication.

Quotations which appear in the text without citation have usually been taken from letters or other unpublished material. However, a few footnotes have been added explaining literary references with which English-speaking readers might not be familiar.

Author's Foreword

In science as in other fields a progressive loss of individuality is taking its course. At the same time, historical perspectives fade. It is as if there were, in the forward press of research activity, no longer time for a backward look. Yet every man knows that the generation of today stands on the shoulders of great predecessors. Understanding of the work of these pioneers, however, becomes too easily assimilated into the anonymous bulk of the past. How their results developed step by step, how personal traits appear in their work, is scarcely asked.

This author has often felt the limitation of historical and human background to be a genuine deprivation. Hence, when a few years ago he was invited by the editor of the series "Grosse Naturforscher," Dr. Heinz Degen (Akademische Verlagsgesellschaft, Stuttgart), to write a biography of Theodor Boveri, the great cytologist of the turn of the last century, he set himself two tasks: to depict this rich personality and to present not only the scientific work itself, but, in so far as possible, the inner trend that the work followed.

This aim had a particular fascination since Boveri belonged to the classical period when cytology and genetics were becoming united into one field; the appeal was all the more powerful because Boveri was not only the discover of fundamental facts, but at the same time the creator of important general concepts that had a far reaching influence on the whole research field. On the other hand, one who has lived during the last decades has become aware of the rapidity with which research fields shift. In the course of a generation after Boveri's death, an extremely large number of new methods have been introduced, such as the refined biochemical techniques and electron microscopy. Last but not least, new organisms have been made available for research, such as the fruit fly *Drosophila*. All this was a challenge to place Boveri's work in perspective in the large historical frame.

The present author first met Boveri in 1905 when, as a student, he came to Boveri's institute at Würzburg to work for the doctorate, and stayed there as assistant and docent until Boveri's death in 1915. The personal relations of those years have remained an indelible memory. In addition, there were letters. Boveri was a spontaneous, highly personal correspondent, fond of humor and blunt sayings. Unfortunately a great part of his correspondence, carefully collected after his death by Frau Marcella Boveri, was lost in the bombardment of Würzburg in the Second World War. This material included almost all the replies to Boveri's own letters. By unusual luck, however, a number of letters written by Boveri to his brother and sister-in-law in Baden, Switzerland, became available. There were also letters to August Pauly, with whom Boveri had formed a close friendship in Munich; to Hans Spemann, one of his first doctoral students, who remained in touch with him; and to W. C. Röntgen, his colleague in physics at Würzburg. I express heartfelt thanks to Dr. Margret Boveri, the daughter of Theodor and Marcella Boveri, and to Kurt Iseman, M.D., the son-in-law of August Pauly, for giving all this private and precious material into my hand.

F.B.

Contents

List of Figures, xiii
Chronology, xv

PART ONE: LIFE AND PERSONALITY

Family and Childhood, 3
Student and Research Years in Munich, 6
Friendship with August Pauly, 8
Illness, 1890, 10
Hertwig's Laboratory and the Call to Würzburg, 13
Marriage, 1897, 15
Later Years and Death, 18
The Scientist, 23
The Institute in Würzburg, 27
Art, Nature, Friends, 41
Naples, 50
Epilogue, 56

PART TWO: SCIENTIFIC WORK

Introduction, 60
I. The Chromosome Studies, 64
The Theory of the Individuality of the Chromosomes, 64
Boveri's Theory of Fertilization, 69

    The Nucleus as Carrier of Heredity, Experiments on the Sea Urchin Egg, Merogonic Hybrids, 76
    The Chromosome Theory of Inheritance, Experiments with Doubly Fertilized Sea Urchin Eggs (Dispermy Experiments), 85
    The Cytological Basis of Mendelian Phenomena, The Boveri-Sutton Theory, 99
II. Investigations of the Constitution of the Egg and the Collaboration of Cytoplasm and Nucleus in Embryonic Development, 105
    On the Structure, Development, and Potencies of the Sea Urchin Egg, 106
    The Problem of Embryonic Differentiation, Analysis of Diminution in the Development of Ascaris, 114
III. Boveri the Comparative Anatomist, 126
IV. Boveri's Views on the Evolution of Living Organisms, 130

REFERENCES

Theodor Boveri's Scientific Publications, 143
Obituary Publications, 147
Citations from Boveri's Scientific Field, 148
Publications from the Zoological Institute of Würzburg (1894–1915), 153

Glossary, 159
Index, 163

List of Figures

FIGURE 1. Mitotic nuclear and cell divisions, 61
FIGURE 2. *Ascaris megalocephala* chromosomes; bivalens race, 65
FIGURE 3. *Ascaris megalocephala* chromosomes; univalens race, 67
FIGURE 4. Fertilization of the sea urchin egg, 71
FIGURE 5. Fertilization in the worm *Sagitta*, 72
FIGURE 6. Tetrapolar spindle in an egg of *Ascaris megalocephala* bivalens, 74
FIGURE 7. Development of fragments of the sea urchin egg fertilized by sperm of the same species, 77
FIGURE 8. Larval types of the sea urchins *Psammechinus* and *Sphaerechinus* and their hybrid, 80
FIGURE 9. Development of dispermic sea urchin eggs, 87
FIGURE 10. Development of pluteus with skeletal defect from a "simultaneous three," 93
FIGURE 11. Diagram of chromosome reduction and Mendelian segregation, 100
FIGURE 12. Development of the sea urchin *Paracentrotus* to the pluteus stage, 108
FIGURE 13. Diminution of chromosomes and development of the egg of *Ascaris megalocephala* univalens, 116
FIGURE 14. Schematic representation of the development of germ line and somatic line in *Ascaris*, 118

FIGURE 15. *Ascaris megalocephala*; normal cleavage, 120
FIGURE 16. *Ascaris megalocephala* univalens; cleavage and diminution of a tetraster egg with two germ lines, 123
FIGURE 17. Nephridial canal of the lancelet *Amphioxus*, 128

Chronology

October 12, 1862. Born in Bamberg, the second of four sons of Theodor Boveri, M.D., and Antonie Boveri, née Elssner.

1868–1875. Attended elementary and Latin schools in Bamberg.

1875–1881. Student at the Realgymnasium, Nürnberg; final examination, 1881.

1881–1885. Studies at the University of Munich, first in historical and philosophical, then in anatomical and biological fields. Dissertation under direction of the anatomist C. von Kupffer: "Contribution to the Knowledge of Nerve Fibers."

1885. Doctorate awarded for the above-mentioned dissertation, *summa cum laude* by the Faculty of Philosophy and Natural Sciences of Munich.

1886–1891. Lamont Fellowship; independent investigation at the Zoological Institute, Munich. First sojourn at the zoological station in Naples.

1887. Inauguration as Lecturer in Zoology and Comparative Anatomy in the Faculty of Philosophy and Natural Sciences of the University of Munich.

1891–1893.	Assistant in the Zoological Institute of the University of Munich, with Richard Hertwig.
1893–1915.	Professor of Zoology and Comparative Anatomy at the University of Würzburg.
1897.	Marriage to Marcella O'Grady of Poughkeepsie, New York, U.S.A.
1900.	Birth of a daughter.
1913.	Refusal of the directorship of the projected Kaiser Wilhelm Institute for Biology in Berlin-Dahlem.
October 15, 1915.	Died in Würzburg.

As the outline shows, Boveri did not live to an advanced age and his exterior life progressed in a limited framework. This sedentary existence contrasts strongly with the qualities of the man himself: his broad human understanding; his wide views; the vital tension of his science; and his generously endowed artistic personality. Clearly the force of these qualities was not matched by a corresponding physical constitution. Boveri, in his own view, was one of those who live at the very limit of their powers.

THEODOR BOVERI

PART ONE:
LIFE AND PERSONALITY

FAMILY AND CHILDHOOD

The name Boveri indicates an Italian origin. In fact, the family goes back to a Carolus Boveri, who immigrated from Savoy and came to Franconia, settling in Iphofen, a tiny Franconian town, about 1590, there marrying Apollonia Lindwurm. From that time on, until the generation of Theodor Boveri, the Boveris married only Franconian wives and presented the province with a series of distinguished jurists. From this origin one can understand the steadfastness of the attachment Theodor Boveri evinced all his life for the Franconian landscape as well as for the University of Würzburg.

In his ancestry we meet respected Franconian burghers. The grandfather on the paternal side, Albert Boveri, was a justice in Bamberg; his wife, née von Bezold, came from Rothenberg, the Franconian town famous for its medieval art. From this side, too, there originate the handsome family portraits and artistic objects of the Empire and Biedermeier period that belong to the family estate. The maternal grandmother, Caroline Schuster, also came from a distinguished Bamberg family. However, the maternal grandfather, Josef Elssner, was a poor farmer's son. Born in the vicinity of Straubing in southern Bavaria, he worked his way up, studied law, and became a highly respected lawyer. For many years he was a member of the Upper Franconian district council.

In the next generation the picture changes. Theodor Boveri, the father of the zoologist, a highly gifted but unstable man, turned to medicine but practised regularly only up to the time of his marriage. He was a forerunner of the naturopathic school which Schweninger later brought into recognition. In regard to biological interests, he was a well-informed botanist, a lover of plants and flowers all his life. His true gifts, however, were artistic. An eminent pianist in his own right, he formed the center of public musical life in Bamberg, and was on personal terms with the best professional artists of his time. He was also distinguished by a considerable talent for drawing.

The mother of the zoologist Theodor Boveri, Antonie, née Elssner, is described to us as an intelligent, energetic woman, mistress of all feminine handicrafts, including the most intricate. As was customary in the period, she also learned painting and music, but abandoned these arts in view of the superior talent of her husband. If the artistic abilities of the son originated mainly from the father, his ethical strength and clear intellectual sense of order came from his mother, his mental acuity and logic from his jurist forbears. Another endowment he may possibly have received from his mother was a remarkable manual dexterity. This found expression in his childhood in the creation of charming imaginative toys and in spontaneous plastic modelling.

At the age of 13, his school days in Bamberg completed, Theodor Boveri was sent to the Realgymnasium at Nürnberg, since his father believed that his talents pointed to architecture or engineering. There his musical gifts were developed by Robert Steuer, the director of the city music school, into whose family the boy was taken. While he grew out of the parental home, he nevertheless spent his holidays with his own family in Bamberg or, especially, in neighbouring Höfen where the Boveris had a country house inherited from the maternal ancestors. In the lovely landscape there young Boveri found the greatest stimulus for his drawing and painting.

A schoolmate, Hermann Beeg, has depicted Boveri in gymnasium days. The traits of the grown man are astonishingly mirrored in the boy, thus underlining the continuity and uniformity with which his character developed. The boy already possessed the man's reserve. He was not a dazzling personality and evidently did not desire to play a brilliant or a leading role in his class, although he could easily have done so by reason of his intellectual gifts, his perceptiveness, and his versatility. One was tempted to "consider his silence as tediousness, his precision of behaviour as pedantry" (57:7). Gradually, as Beeg further reports, his schoolboy friends realized that this Boveri was no careerist or grind, as they thought at first; that he took time outside of school for many diversions, for music, drawing, and painting; that this reserved boy was a young man of flesh and blood like themselves, and what is more, quite the devil of a fellow. He did not haunt the instructors, even those he admired. His distaste for public attention was compensated by an objective self-criticism, which guarded him from overestimating his own abilities and allowed him to give full value to the achievements of others.

To his great endowments was added even then another characteristic that remained with him all his life, and that we as students later discovered in him. This was an extraordinary carefulness, a feeling of responsibility to whatever object concerned him, a conscientiousness that left no stone unturned to complete an undertaking once accepted. This was true for the boy even in studies, such as mathematics, that he disliked.

Corresponding to his distaste for pomposity, Beeg continues, was Boveri's manner of speech; he had a dry style, a factual manner of delivery without "the gift of brilliant diction, somewhat monotonous, but always clear and convincing." In discussion, however, his superiority was striking. No fellow student could resist his judicious logic. "When the others were discussing hotly, contesting over sophistries in excited language, he would often decide the dispute with a dry, even drastic and blunt observation, in such fashion that each contestant was forced by prudence to take in sail" (57:7). Bluntness was characteristic of him all his life.

Boveri preserved throughout life an extraordinarily lively sympathy for music and the fine arts. The buildings and the historical character of Bamberg and Nürnberg made a deep impression on the growing boy. The cathedral of Bamberg, that great example of romanesque architecture, was perforce especially dear to him. Failure to visit the cathedral when one was a guest at Höfen marked a person in his eyes as artistically insensible. Gross ignorance in the elements of art, too, was a direct provocation. When a fellow-student referred to a romanesque capital as an ancient Roman construction, Boveri angrily shouted at him, "Are you really such a stupid ass as not to know the difference between Roman and romanesque?" (57:10).

Student and Research Years in Munich

At the end of his years at the gymnasium, his qualifying examinations completed with distinction, Boveri entered the University of Munich in 1881 and devoted himself first to the curriculum of historical-philosophical studies. This area of scholarship presupposed a classical background, which had not been available at the Realgymnasium. Boveri therefore mastered Greek in the brief period of nine months; he had learned Latin at Bamberg. He passed the special qualifying examinations for humanistic studies, again with distinction. This feat of productive energy won him, in addition to the classical foundation he needed, the good fortune of a place in the Maximilianeum.[1] This residence for outstanding alumni of Bavarian gymnasia, the "genius sty" in frivolous Munich parlance, afforded Boveri free board and lodging

[1] The Maximilianeum was originally founded as a training center for pages of the royal court with, under the same roof, a very small number of places for the highest ranking graduates of Bavarian gymnasia who were thus provided with university scholarships. In pre-1914 days, since alumni of the Maximilianeum went on to important academic and government posts, this common personal background had considerable influence in shaping official policy.

for the period of his studies — a fortunate dispensation since the material circumstances of the family were visibly becoming critical. The state residence also fulfilled his need for beauty. From the roof of the Maximilianeum he had one of the finest panoramic views of Munich. "No king can live more splendidly in the royal palace than Boveri in his," one of his friends wrote at the time.

At the end of a semester Boveri changed from the historical area to natural science. He first turned to anatomy, becoming for a time assistant in the Anatomical Institute at Munich with Carl von Kupffer. The reason was beyond doubt largely financial. He needed to become independent as soon as possible. A further consideration was that anatomy left the road open to practical medicine, should scientific research fail him as a career. At the Anatomical Institute he wrote, under the direction of von Kupffer, his dissertation "Contributions to the Knowledge of Nerve Fibers," which, in 1885, was submitted to the Faculty of Philosophy and Natural Sciences of Munich for the degree of Doctor of Philosophy. Boveri always retained great devotion for Carl von Kupffer, "his fatherly adviser and friend," and in 1899 dedicated to him, on the occasion of his 60th birthday, one of the finest studies on *Ascaris*.

The decisive turn to biology came in the spring of 1885, when Boveri was awarded the Lamont Fellowship by the Faculty of Philosophy and Natural Sciences of Munich, at first for five, then for two additional years. Seldom has a scholarship been more fruitfully used. Boveri could now dedicate himself freely to research. He gave up his assistantship in anatomy and settled into the Zoological Institute in 1885, welcomed kindly by Richard Hertwig. Twenty-five years later, in an address on the occasion of Hertwig's 60th birthday (Hertwig, 1910), Boveri recalled his reception there. "It was in the beginning of May, 1885, only a few days after your own arrival in Munich, that I presented myself to you, up in your laboratory, as a research fellow. When I told you that I wished to work full time and begged you to assign me a place, you, after a little consideration, cleared off the table in front of you, told me to take the other end, and thus we conveyed the table to the next room, where I was able to start work at once." This institute, later one of the largest in Europe, consisted at that time of only seven rooms. There was in general no working space for research fellows. In the address, Boveri designated himself as a student of Hertwig, who inducted him into the field of cytology. He nevertheless struck out on his own at once. The great work of Eduard van Beneden, published in 1883, exercised a decisive influence. The series of chromosome studies to be delineated in the second part of this memoir began at the institute in Munich.

Friendship with August Pauly

During his first years at Munich, Boveri struck up a close friendship with August Pauly which, in spite of occasional vehement differences of opinion, continued as a vital force until Pauly's death in 1914.

At the time of their meeting, Pauly was 35 and Boveri 23. In spite of the difference in age, they had in common a serious devotion to science, great affection for art as well as for nature, and an unusual directness of mind. Both tended to enjoy rural and primitive life as well as blunt humor.

Pauly,[2] a spirited, intensely stimulating personality, radiated a powerful attraction. Entirely on his own, he had achieved a rare personal culture which, besides his biological interests, embraced the philosophical and especially the artistic aspects of human life. In addition, he was poetically gifted. Intellect and feeling, subjective intuition and scientific method, were blended and balanced in his character. Pauly's family origin also was out of the ordinary, and not academic. He had had a difficult childhood. The father, by occupation first a smith, then an innkeeper, was a hot-blooded, irascible native of the south of France; the mother was Bavarian. In the son an urge to reach insight and truth was united with his father's irrepressible temperament and the quiet intensity of his mother's spirit.

[2] The following sketch of Pauly originates in H. Spemann's autobiography (1948); Spemann was a close friend of Pauly.

With Boveri's move to the Zoological Institute, he and Pauly became associates, seeing one another every day. Pauly was assistant there and also *Privatdozent* in zoology. Later, in 1896, he took over the chair of forest zoology. What this friendship meant to Boveri was epitomized by him in a letter dated May 18, 1905. "Every day now I recall the spring 20 years ago when we worked side by side at the anatomy table and became friends. Since this is a sort of anniversary, let me for once say how much happiness, what precious memories this friendship has brought and does bring to me." On the other hand, Pauly, older and burdened with a hypersensitive spirit, had need of his younger, more harmonious friend. "In order to live, man always needs a fellow-man," he once wrote.

At once, sooner than other colleagues, Pauly was fascinated by Boveri's talents. He kept a sort of journal about his younger friend. These entries, together with numerous letters from Boveri, give us a lively and personal picture of those years, so decisive for Boveri. Pauly writes on February 24, 1885, that Boveri gave him the manuscript of his dissertation to read. "I expected a dry histological work with minute details, and found instead something admirable. The paper, every word and every part is remarkably thought through, intelligent throughout, and mature. All this from native talent, unstrained, effortless. One seldom reads such good writing by a young author. It shows extraordinarily sharp microscopic observation, and an equally acute perception of the essential."

From then on Pauly followed Boveri's ascent with lively and ungrudging sympathy. This good will was as a matter of fact not superfluous. In the face of ambitious and grasping academic competitors Boveri had no defense.

At the end of November, 1887, Boveri underwent his *Habilitation*, qualifying as university lecturer. He later became a most distinguished speaker and, on special occasions such as his induction into the Rectorship at Würzburg or his memorial address for Anton Dohrn at Graz, an impressive orator. Nevertheless,

Pauly at the time was not happy about his friend's maiden lecture before the faculty. Though he found the content good, Boveri's delivery was in his view "not dashing enough. He omits even permissible rhetorical effects." On the other hand, in discussion, the keen logician emerged. "Hertwig, who moved to the attack [his duty as academic sponsor], was so decisively defeated that the audience beamed." In other cases, too, Pauly made similar criticisms of Boveri. "What I should wish," he wrote a year later after hearing a lecture by Boveri, "would be a bit more liveliness in every sense." This judgment corresponds strikingly with the description cited previously by Boveri's schoolmate.

From January until the end of April, 1888, and again in the spring of 1889, Boveri went to Naples to work at the zoological station founded by Anton Dohrn. During his first three years in Munich he had studied the behavior of the chromosomes in the egg of the roundworm of the horse (*Ascaris megalocephala*) and had based his theory of the individuality of the chromosomes on these observations. His first sojourn in Naples yielded him material demonstrating the equivalence of the chromosome sets in sperm and egg; the second visit he employed in working out the famous merogony experiment.

Illness, 1890

In spite of the deliberateness of his approach, Boveri's talent was of the early maturing variety. In these beginning years, following the intrinsic lead of his research and disregarding his health, he created the foundation of his whole life's work. All that we shall describe in the second part of this book, the identification of the chromosomes as protagonists of heredity and the antagonistic role of the cytoplasm, had its inception in the work of these early years.

In 1890, however, Boveri's health was severely shaken, and for a long period he was unable to work. Several circumstances contributed. As the following years indicate, his health really was unequal to the intensity with which he worked; in addition, his family caused him the most acute anxieties. His father had dissipated the means of the once well-to-do family and had brought it deeply into debt. A sick man, he was completely inaccessible to the pleas and remonstrances of his sons. Moreover, the health of the mother, with whom the son was very close, was shaken by these events. The main burden of the whole situation, discussions with the father as well as financial settlements with the creditors, lay on Theodor, since his brother Walter was working in Switzerland. His conduct of affairs is witness to his inherent moral fortitude and to his extraordinary objectivity. "It is a question for you and me," he wrote to Walter[3] in March, 1890, "whether we as brothers will be able to prevent the complete collapse of the estate, which under the present circumstances can scarcely be delayed half a year." The catastrophe was actually avoided by the efforts of the sons and the cooperation of the creditors. For Theodor Boveri, all this was a very heavy burden which, together with his own illness, seriously endangered his scientific career. His sickness was originally explained as an innocuous influenza, later developing into what Boveri himself recognized as a severe neurasthenia. It forced him, from the middle of 1890 until the summer of 1891, to renounce all work. Periods of health alternated with deep depressions.

At first, in order to arrange the family affairs, he lived in Bamberg with his parents. He then went briefly to Munich, found it intolerable, and finally landed in a sanatorium in Constance. Letters inform us of his condition. "You probably have heard," he wrote ironically to Walter, "that in suffering from the after-effects of an influenza I am about half a year out of fashion. I am still not recovered; my brain in particular seems frozen, and mental activity, which at present includes even writing letters, is forbidden me. The basic symptom is weakness in every respect.

[3] Walter Boveri was then engaged as an electrotechnician in the Oerlikon machine factory in Zurich. In 1891 he married Victoire Baumann, with whom Theodor Boveri exchanged many letters; in the same year W. Boveri founded, jointly with the Englishman C. E. L. Brown, the present international firm of Brown, Boveri and Co., at Baden, Aargau.

The doctors claim to find nothing wrong beyond anemia. Apparently it frequently happens that people fail to recover after influenza — rather poor consolation." Similarly, to his future sister-in-law, he wrote, "I am *so* completely gone to the dogs (if this expression is not familiar to you, Walter will explain) that I can make no decisions and end up completely stupified. Walking strains my legs, reading my eyes, writing my brain; in short, any activity is too great an exertion, and so I sit or lie about, evoking mentally as many disagreeable things as possible, and depicting them to myself in rich black tones." And a month later, again to his brother, from Munich: "I've been here since yesterday evening and am feeling so unhappy, wandering about like the village idiot in a place where for nine years I had been used to doing real work, that I wish to leave as soon as possible."

Subsequent events in the family were not of a nature to expedite recovery. On January 4, 1891, still in Munich, he received a telegram. His father was on his deathbed. Boveri "stayed with me in my room," writes Pauly, "and we talked over the bad news. Although his father, out of pure folly, . . . had squandered his whole estate, there was a strong attachment; the father was not malicious, only wrongheaded. Boveri will go home to Bamberg this afternoon and continue to a neurological sanatorium as soon as everything is arranged at home." The death of his father was on the whole a relief.

On February 25 of the same year his brother Walter was married. The letter that Theodor Boveri wrote on this occasion from Constance is characteristic of the depth of his nature and the painful burden of his illness.

> Never before in these seven months that I have passed in enforced idleness have I felt my malady so deeply as just today. You understand how dismal it will be for me to have to spend tomorrow with indifferent strangers. In particular, since no one else of our family can be there, I feel that I am neglecting a duty in not coming, and each renewed invitation of yours has made it more difficult to obey the orders of the doctors. But I must. If I could be with you tomor-

row I should probably not convey my good wishes more expressively than by a handshake or by the kiss I have been promised. On paper, too, it is not my way to use many words. Bless you and be happy.

Finally, after another four months, Boveri began to improve, although the phrase about "being gone to the dogs" lingered as a lifelong refrain. He remained a man susceptible to illness, suffering particularly from protracted rheumatic attacks. He returned to Munich for the winter semester, 1891.

HERTWIG'S LABORATORY AND THE CALL TO WURZBURG

In 1891 Boveri's Lamont Fellowship expired. In the summer of that year he succeeded Pauly in the assistantship at the Zoological Institute at Munich, under Richard Hertwig. This assumption of duties was largely caused by his critical financial status: scientifically he had far outgrown such a position. For four years he had been *Privatdozent*; as a cytologist he belonged among the leaders. Lectures and laboratory teaching had extended his experience to the most diverse fields. Finally, the criticism that might have hampered his academic career, namely, that his research was too specialized, was disproved by his discovery in 1890 of the nephridia of *Amphioxus* (13-15). This last demonstrated a major talent for comparative anatomy.

The extent of his international repute was shown by the foreign scientists he attracted who wished to work with him even though he was still Hertwig's assistant — a novelty in the hierarchy of the institute. With genuine pride Boveri wrote at the time to his sister-in-law that an American professor (E. B. Wilson, later the dean of cytologists in the U.S.A.) and another special student from Paris were to work with him. "With the latter, who knows practically no German, I speak an atrocious French." With Wilson he formed a lasting friendship.

But his future still remained uncertain. Several prospects for a permanent position emerged, but came to nothing. He turned down a lecturership in cytology at Clark University, in Massachusetts. An associate position in the zoological division of the museum in Munich did indeed offer prospects of a secure existence, but would have led him away from the field of his greatest talents, which were in the direction of general biology.

At this point, unexpectedly, a new prospect opened. Pauly wrote on October 18, 1892, "I have rarely been so excited by happy news as I was by what Boveri told me when I entered his room. It seems that the chair of zoology in Würzburg will be free sooner than expected. Sachs[4] has written Goebel inquiring about Boveri, and of course Goebel has passed the question on to Hertwig. How splendid if he should really get a professorship! Nothing has stirred for so long — as if fate had been sleeping." This time, however, fate did not sleep. On January 1, 1893, Pauly noted, "When I went to see Boveri, he had excellent news: a letter from Sachs himself, telling him of the vacancy of Semper's chair. Sachs wishes to propose Boveri's name to the Ministry as first-ranking candidate, and asked him for a list of his publications. Naturally we talked of nothing else. My delight at his luck is great, and would be greater if I were not holding it in check for fear of some unforseen disappointment."

Instead, one happy event followed another. On January 26, Boveri had another letter from Sachs, telling him that his election was assured. On February 6, he was invited to present himself to the Minister. For this occasion, as he reported in an amusing letter to his sister-in-law in Baden, dated January 30, he was already provided. "I am certainly not given to optimism, but after this letter from Sachs and in view of the general situation, I considered the affair decided, and ordered a handsome frock coat, trousers, and vest from a tailor for the presentation. This acquisition even enticed me to go to a ball — something I have not done for seven years — albeit for only two hours. The position in Würzburg is in every way desirable; in particular the institute is handsome and excellently equipped. It is quite new, just finished in 1889."

[4] Von Sachs was Professor of Botany in Würzburg, Goebel in Munich.

On March 22, 1893, Boveri at the age of 30 was called to the position of Professor of Zoology and Comparative Anatomy, and Director of the Zoological-Zootomical Institute of the University of Würzburg. Würzburg thus gained one of the foremost biologists of the period. For Boveri, the election was one of the decisive events of his life. His research career was now assured. He was to remain loyal to Würzburg and to his Franconian homeland until the end of his life. The extremely favorable turn of affairs did not prevent another severe attack of neurasthenia, even at the time of assuming his new position. Boveri lived in fear of not being able to fulfil his new duties. "He has not yet regained his strength," noted Pauly, "and feels unfortunate in the midst of his good fortune." The two friends then went for a few days to Lake Starnberg to pass the time in painting, walking, resting, looking at insects, chatting about the art of lecturing and about politics. On this occasion Pauly gave his friend, who was faced with lecturing on insects during the coming semester, an introduction to entomology.

Marriage, 1897

A student first meeting Boveri in his later years was confronted with a poised personality, restrained in expression, betraying little of his inner self, one who, notwithstanding a lively sense of humour, regarded life with a certain resignation. In his younger years, however, he was high spirited and open to all aspects of life. He expressed himself with particular freedom to Victoire Boveri, the young wife of his brother Walter, in the matter of his affairs of the heart. In his early 30's, he began pondering the problem of marriage; naturally there were relatives who hoped to marry him off. A cousin had invited him to meet a niece of his, supposing that she would suit him as a life partner. "What she says and does," Boveri wrote to his sister-in-law in 1892, "is all pleasing to me. She plays the piano very well and paints even better. In short, she is thoroughly sympathetic to me. But the wish to be married to her did not occur to me for an instant, and after all, that point has some importance." In view of his own uncertain health, he must have hesitated over the fragile constitution of the young person.

The thought of marriage continued to preoccupy him. "In that circle," he continued, "was a girl whom I liked very much. There was, I believe, a feeling of mutual sympathy." There follows the sketch of a little love scene comparable to the bean romance in Gottfried Keller's *Green Henry*. Making music together was an important element.

Boveri's intentions were serious. "The father is Justice of the Court of Appeals here, an old friend of Steuer. I have already paid a call; we'll see how it goes. But say nothing to Mama or anyone else." A month later, to the same correspondent: "The affair appears doubtful to you? At present the risk is not great. If things really were to progress so far that I should decide to marry her — and vice versa N. B., which remains a great question — it might not be so bad. Naturally this presupposes a regular university position. If only one can manage tolerably, and bring up his children decently, that is the main thing. If the children are *daughters* and are without great financial expectations, well, it is better that they remain unmarried than to be taken for their money; if they are *sons*, and want to be rich, it is their own business to find well-to-do wives. I don't see why I should undertake that for them. But in any case, these are pure fantasies."

Later, though one prerequisite was filled by the professorship at Würzburg, no marriage resulted from this inclination. Fate led in another direction. In 1896 an American student of E. B. Wilson's came to Würzburg to work with Boveri. This was Marcella Imelda O'Grady, a professor at Vassar College. She aroused his interest, although he claimed to be opposed to higher learning for women. "I now have," he wrote to his sister-in-law, "an American lady zoologist in the institute; she is not really pretty, but quite attractive. I enjoy her company and must sometimes restrain myself: I think she does not care for frivolity." Two months later he wrote, "I have invited my American student, with whom I have in the meantime become good friends, for a few days at Höfen, to Mama's alarm; I don't know if she will really come." During this so-to-speak critical period he underwent a severe bout of rheumatism that crippled his right arm temporarily and necessitated a stay and treatment in a clinic. "This is all I need to complete my neurasthenia. It is now six years that I have been good for nothing and it looks as if this were to go on without end. . . . My American student visits me occasionally; Mama's anxiety has already been aroused by this friendship."

In fact, Miss O'Grady was, personally and scientifically, becoming more and more at home in Würzburg. "Everyone strives," Boveri himself wrote in December, 1896, not without humor, "to be agreeable to her. The scientific world of Würzburg has been highly exercised by her question, whether she might be introduced as a guest at the meetings of the illustrious Physico–Medical Society. Overwhelming majority in favor." The excitement aroused in academic quarters by Miss O'Grady's request proved that as far as the emancipation of women was concerned the views of the university community lagged far behind those of their young American guest.

Six months later, on June 13, 1897, Boveri informed his sister-in-law in Baden that he was "really and truly" engaged to Miss O'Grady. And the same Boveri who had earlier written that he was no friend of long engagements, found it now much more charming than he had expected, "although rather exciting." The marriage took place October 5, 1897, in Boston.

As a zoologist, Frau Boveri took active part in the scientific work of her husband. The investigation that she began in his laboratory dealt with experimental sea urchin eggs in which the sperm nucleus was connected with only one of the cleavage asters. She published the results in 1903 under the title "Concerning Mitoses with Unilateral Chromosome Attachments." This work gave her familiarity with sea urchin development, and hence the experience that stood her in good stead as her husband's collaborator in many joint investigations. She shared his joy and satisfaction in successful experiments and his sorrows in failure.

Quite outside of scientific matters, Marcella Boveri was, in health and in illness, a devoted and encouraging life partner to her husband, "with a clear mind, a quiet spirit, and, not least, with a warm heart" (Röntgen). One cannot say that the marriage was without problems. In Frau Boveri's character, in addition to scientific interests, was a rationalistic and also a puritanical strain, allied to her generous and energetic helpfulness. In contrast, Theodor Boveri's life, complementing his research, was artistic and sensuous.

In 1900 a daughter was born to them. "Since the little thing delayed almost four weeks before she finally decided to enter the world," he wrote Pauly on August 16, 1900, "it was not a speedy passage from water to land life; and I cannot describe to you the patience and courage shown by my dear wife, nor what I lived through for two nights and days. It was enough to expiate a multitude of sins. She is happy to be able to nurse the child herself; the little one works resolutely with her large mouth. I cannot say that I feel very paternal as yet, though I follow with great interest the various psychic manifestations and changes apparent after only two days." When the first month was past, he went to Höfen for six days "to recover a bit from becoming a father." A very close relationship grew up between him and the daughter. It was later a charming picture to see the little Margret come to her father in the institute with her projects, to model, draw, saw, or hammer.

Later Years and Death

In the spring of 1910 Boveri's mother died at the age of 67. Their close relationship is clear from his active solicitude and sympathy for her during her illness at the time of his father's death. The son always returned for comfort to his mother's house in Bamberg, as well as to Höfen, where she lived during the summer. He often recovered from his illnesses in her care. It is easy to understand that she contemplated his marriage to an American with an anxious heart. "As far as Mama is concerned," he wrote at the time to his brother in Baden, "she recognized the news of my engagement by the outside of my letter, namely by its thickness (two double sheets!), and she was so paralyzed with terror that she scarcely could open it. She replied accordingly, and I therefore went to see her on Ascension Thursday to calm her a bit." She subsequently received her daughter-in-law in the most friendly manner.

In later years, when Boveri had his own family, mother and son remained close. He expressed his grief at her death to a young woman friend, a former student with whom he had remained in touch. "The death of my mother, whom I had hoped to keep with me for many more years, has affected me severely, and I feel suddenly old. I seem to have lived through pretty much everything, and I regard the story as essentially finished. But perhaps such moods will pass." His mother was one of those figures of whom he once wrote, in another connection, "Even when one almost never sees a beloved person, the knowledge of his existence, his belonging to oneself, gives a feeling of richness. He extends the root system by which we are attached to humanity, in breadth and depth. All this dies with the beloved."

At the turn of the century Boveri was internationally known as a biologist. Distinction multiplies responsibilities. He experienced the increasing weight of university business in the faculty, senate, and administration. There, as in matters of appointments, his careful and objective judgement was often requested. Offers of positions in other institutions he found disquieting and troublesome. He rejected some of these calls, such as that to Leipzig, in preliminary stages. Others attracted him more, as in the case of the call to Freiburg in Breisgau in 1911. "It might be a temptation of Pescara,"[5] he wrote to Spemann, "though it would not now be painful for my wife and me to leave Würzburg. Most of those close to us have left. And if I should see that I can set

[5] The allusion is to the novel of C. F. Meyer, *Die Versuchung des Pescara*.

myself up comfortably there (in Freiburg) I might decide, in my old age, to begin again as *homo novus*." But a month later he wrote that he had "after long inner struggles finally decided to remain in his native land."

This decision had scarcely been taken when a stronger temptation appeared: the offer of the directorship of the newly projected Kaiser Wilhelm Institute for Biology in Berlin-Dahlem. The attraction was the new concept of an institute of purely research character, free of teaching obligations. This institute was one of the first to be established by the Kaiser Wilhelm Foundation for free research and cooperation among different biological disciplines. Letters to Spemann inform us of the ups and downs of the dealings, so fundamentally agonizing for Boveri. The situation, he wrote to Spemann on March 27, 1912, was at first tangled, a "delicious confusion of aspirations and intrigues. One group seems to want me. Oskar Hertwig wants Haecker, Roux' candidate is Herbst." The decision finally was for Boveri. "Recently (this is strictly confidential!!!) Schmidt-Ott, the director of the Berlin Ministry, came to see me concerning the Institute of the Kaiser Wilhelm Foundation. Things seem to have progressed to the extent that I can have the position [of Director] if I wish it. But do I and should I wish it? There are days when everything in prospect there seems easy and attractive, and other days when I find it flatly senseless to leave this place where things are to my liking." This emotional contradiction, which made decisions difficult for him, is an essential trait. It probably derived from the tendency to depression and the doubts about his physical capabilities and these in turn were a consequence of his frequent illnesses. He gradually was coming to resemble, he wrote Spemann at the time, "that chandelier mentioned by Lichtenberg which, even though it had ceased to give light, nevertheless decorated the room."

The negotiations were lengthy. He had not only to decide if he himself would undertake the direction of the whole institute, but also what research fields in zoology should be represented by independent departments, and which investigators should be entrusted with the direction of these departments. After long study, he proposed Max Hartmann for the Department of Protozoology, Richard Goldschmidt for Animal Genetics, Hans Spemann for Developmental Physiology, and Otto Warburg for the Department of Biochemistry. These choices were made in 1912, and were put into effect even after Boveri had refused the directorship of the institute for himself. The men chosen were young scientists at the time. Their selection shows the accuracy, depth, and breadth of Boveri's judgement, since all became scientists of the first rank, two of them Nobel laureates. But the sensitive Boveri had expended some of his own health in the decisions.

"I am," he wrote to Spemann on January 27, 1913, "at the end of my forces. For four months this inner struggle has torn me and you cannot conceive what all has fallen on my shoulders in this period." Toward the end of the negotiations he fell victim to a fairly severe illness with slight paralysis of the right side of the body. This, in addition to the difficulties of the negotiations in Berlin, settled his decision to refuse the position. The doctors, including the internist Krehl, had not offered objections from the medical point of view. "But I could clearly gather from his [Krehl's] words that it would be better for me to remain in Würzburg and not to expose myself to the Berlin atmosphere. The main point is that I myself feel this to be true. Naturally it is with a heavy heart that I give up this undertaking, to which I had thought myself so firmly committed, and it is of special regret to renounce the happy prospect of living in daily contact with you, as in old days." Nevertheless, after the decision was made, it seemed to him as if "at the last moment a guardian angel had held him back."

In the beginning of August, 1914, the First World War broke out. Boveri believed, although not entirely without reservation, that the German cause was justified. He could not understand the critical attitude of several of the German Swiss. He was fundamentally bourgeois-conservative. In his mind the meaning of "heritage" and "ownership" was coupled with the consciousness of responsibility (Margret Boveri, 1960). Although he had always fought shy of politics, he had been in close touch with government offices in his position as Senator and Rector of the university. Soon, knowing the tenacity of the Anglo-Saxons, he became very troubled about the future of his country. Owing to the state of his health he was obliged to follow the course of events in complete inactivity; excitement and anxiety weighed upon him all the more heavily. Two passages from letters to Spemann show Boveri's concern. On August 3, 1914, he wrote, "How enviable these days is a man like Enderlen, [the Würzburg surgeon then called to the front, who, a year later, was to operate on Boveri] who will rush from one serious operation to another. For the first time I really feel the oppression of my physical weakness." Then, on May 4, 1915, five months before his death, he wrote,

> My wife has from the beginning maintained that the war has made me ill, and perhaps there is something in it. So many people are dying unexpectedly these days. I consider it quite possible that violent emotions can cause latent processes to erupt. Dying of a broken heart seems to me to belong in this category. I admit that good news from the war theater could restore my health. There is a wonderful greatness in this struggle of our people for existence.

He adds in a somewhat skeptical tone, "I am almost ready to believe all the good things that H. S. Chamberlain says of us."

Two months later the question of removal of the gall bladder was raised. The operation was postponed for the time being. In the interval of moving to Kissingen for further treatment, Boveri spent ten days at home in Würzburg. "It is noteworthy," he wrote, again to Spemann, "that, since my return to Franconia my temperature, which has been running very high for five months, has suddenly returned to near normal. From this I draw hope that we may make shift to patch up the clattering old machine again. Nevertheless, the evening is coming on and I am thinking of reading the things that everyone should be familiar with. In the winter I started with the Book of Books. Here the New Testament is occupying me, along with Harnack's *What is Christianity?*" On August 19, the diseased gall bladder, with a stone, was excised. In September he reported: "How I am doing, I myself do not exactly know. I still have my inflamed pleura, and the pleura its fever." He died, exchausted, October 15, 1915, three days after his 53rd birthday. The precise nature of his illness is uncertain. His ashes were placed in the family vault in Bamberg. His will provided that no elaborate ceremonies be observed. Before his death he wrote to his brothers that they should all come together after his cremation to be *gemütlich*, to eat, laugh, and indulge in bad jokes.

The Scientist

The natural sciences are considered impersonal; the pioneer figures, however outstanding, are overshadowed by the facts they have established. It is as if scientific research, in its impetus, had no time to concern itself with the personalities of its creators. Yet the work is very often stamped with the character of its maker. This was the case with Boveri.

His mind and the nature of his work were portrayed soon after his death, most profoundly in the memorial volume (57) which appeared in 1918. This volume contains scientific and personal appreciations by Spemann, E. B. Wilson, Wilhelm Wien, this author, and other friends. Since its publication, nearly half a century has passed. Times have altered, general biology and its methods of investigation have profoundly changed their direction. Nevertheless, most of Boveri's contributions remain as enduring possessions of biology; his theoretical concepts have influenced the development of cytology and genetics for decades beyond his death. This will be seen in detail in the discussion of his research. In this chapter we wish only to outline the general features of his scientific character.

There are, among the great biologists, investigators with theoretical gifts who start with abstract ideas and theories, and others who start with the object itself. In the first group one may place

Hans Driesch and August Weismann. For Driesch, vitalistic hypotheses formed the center; for Weismann, the concept of determinants. With the great comparative anatomists, naturally, the anatomical material to be compared preceded its conceptualization. The geneticist T. H. Morgan, who revealed the significance of the fruit fly *Drosophila* in experimental genetics, must also be reckoned in the second group. Boveri stands between the two types. An avowedly visually oriented individual, he was not attracted by the abstract. "It did not suit him," reported Wien, his colleague in physics, "to work with abstract concepts, as would be required by mathematics or systematic philosophy" (57:131). Rather, observation and experimental analysis of *visible* processes formed the point of departure for his scientific work; individual phenomena, however, interested him only when he could put them in a larger context. The field of cell research offered him this concreteness and basic significance that he needed during those decades of creative work.

An important part of the science of genetics is based on the analysis of visible cellular processes, such as the knowledge of the germ cells and the constancy of the chromosomes. That the objects here dealt with are visible only in the microscope does not alter the principle; for Boveri the microscopic *picture* is the point of departure, that is to say, a visible condition or process and not an abstract idea. To be sure, he quickly passed beyond this purely visual beginning to dynamic considerations. His aim was to investigate not individual morphological structures, but the physiological relation between cell structure and cell function: the relation between chromosomes, cytoplasm, and heredity. Boveri thus became one of the pioneers of the principle that the *structure* of protoplasm, including the chromosomes, is one of the irreducible fundamentals of the living process.

To the use of purely physical methods he raised the objection that thereby the framing of biological problems must necessarily "become dependent on the mode of thinking in physics." He expressed this view in opposition to his colleague Wien (57:150).

His position regarding purely chemical methods was similar. He was, of course, like the physicists and the chemists, thoroughly committed to an experimental approach, but as a biologist he preferred the experimental possibilities offered by the living material itself, without artificial challenge. "The investigator of living processes will make it his special concern to find out abnormalities, in which he has not intervened with his crude methods, where he can however penetrate into the nature of the alteration" (43:216).

Cytology since those days has achieved great successes with extremely fine microchemical and physical methods, results that would be unthinkable without these new techniques. At the same time it has become plain how remote lies the goal of true understanding of vital phenomena. Not long ago even so biochemically oriented and so successful an investigator as Jean Brachet (1957:464) called attention to this difficulty. We shall encounter this problem later on several occasions. It is astonishing and especially indicative of Boveri's farsightedness that his theories laid the ground for these new developments.

The great foresight with which Boveri proceeded in his own area of research is clear from the way in which he delimited, in principle, the value of a theory. For any hypothesis, however great, comprehensive, or original, its accessibility to demonstration must be the measure of its value. He expressed this in a lecture before the German Zoological Society in Würzburg in 1903 (32, 34) in the following impressive phrases, here somewhat abbreviated: "Everyone who has followed the history of our science during the past 20 years recognizes immediately and gratefully the value, indeed the indispensibility, of the construction of a consistent hypothetical picture to be fully realized perhaps only in the distant future. Theoretical castles in the air give a powerful stimulus to very laborious detailed investigations. However, in evaluating true progress we must be clear in our minds how far observation and experiment in themselves can take us at this time. To measure this extent is the principal task of the presentation that is to follow. I certainly do not," he concludes, "in thus setting limits, wish to relinquish the aura of hypothetical thought, without which any body of facts remains lifeless" (34:iv). One may realize the importance of so critical an attitude on the part of a leading investigator in that period when many biological circles still refused to accept the existence of chromosomes.

Let us now recapitulate the characteristic traits of Boveri's scientific personality.

First: the elements of his character are reflected in his work: his veracity, acuity, and clarity; his imaginativeness and the independence of his judgment.

Item: his penetrating, thorough observation with the microscope was complemented by deeply thoughtful interpretation. Nothing was overlooked and apparent exceptions were valued as a possible source of new discoveries.

Item: audacity and originality in design of experiments mark him as a master. In the background of all the empirical facts, theoretical concepts and far-reaching ideas continually led him from one step to the next without ever losing touch with the ground. Counterpoised against the dynamic plan was a pervasive balance in judgment and a patience that could wait until the material was ripe for final deductions, often after long years.

Finally, his own judicial pondering was deepened by thorough critical exchange of views with other scientists. These discussions, very unmodern in their completeness, contributed much to the general elucidation and development of problems in that period. Boveri could be a formidable opponent in critical discussions. Sometimes cutting, he was for the most part measured in his expression, a restraint not exactly innate in his temperament. This latter appeared in his often robustly phrased handwritten marginal comments that the doctoral students could read in the reprints sent him by his opponents. His sensitivity in questions of priority, often noted, sometimes justified, was probably based less on ambition than on his passion for clear delimitations.

LIFE AND PERSONALITY

This account of the scientist Boveri would be incomplete without an evaluation of the form of his writings. Their mastery lies in clarity of language, perhaps even more in his artistic illustration. Drawing was a delight for him; writing, he maintained, was torture. In his earlier works he himself prepared all drawings complete for the engraver; in later ones he gave the artist an exact sketch. He disliked photographic reproduction. In his opinion, drawings, in addition to compelling more precise analysis on the part of the observer, accomplished a more effective synthesis. His drawings unite the most accurate representation with the magic of living material. Spemann has correctly observed that at that time Boveri's drawings "made us more accurate, so that he raised the whole level" (66:17).

THE INSTITUTE IN WURZBURG

In the natural sciences the investigator does not work alone; he forms, with "his institute" — with his laboratory and fellow workers — a living unity. As in a workshop, the cooperation may, according to the character of the master, be close or loose; in Würzburg it was very close. Boveri stamped *his* character on the institute. Let us look at it as it was around 1900. The Zoological Institute of Würzburg had developed into an international research institution where doctoral candidates worked side by side with experienced scientists. In particular, numerous Americans who sought to become familiar with Boveri's field came to work in his laboratory. These were the years when Spemann, one of the first of Boveri's students, was still active in Würzburg as docent. The present author, as doctoral candidate, then as assistant and docent until Boveri's death, was also there in that period.

If a modern biologist today should ask how this institute, so influential by reason of a single personality, was organized, the answer must be that even for that remote period it was rather primitive. We had good microscopes, incubators, microtomes, and later a freezing microtome, a centrifuge, and a Tschachotin ultraviolet radiation apparatus. But for a long time there was neither photomicrographic equipment, nor a projection apparatus for instruction, nor, except for the institute preparator, any technical personnel. Everyone had to manage his technical work for himself. Photomicrography was introduced by Spemann, who needed it for his experiments on newt eggs and on toads. Boveri himself had no desire in that direction. He drew; and for precise reproduction, he simply used the Abbé *camera lucida*. Contrary to some other opinions, he maintained, reasonably, that in microscopy (with light optics) the procedure of drawing guarantees the best training, the most accurate analysis, and also the best self-criticism. Consequently, the doctoral students drew, and drew incessantly. Our chief was also basically of the opinion that the best way for a beginner to learn scientific method was to carry through an accurate microscopic analysis.

A further unexpected peculiarity of Boveri's was associated with this preference for delicate microscopic work. Although biology is the science of the living and Boveri himself was one of the most gifted experimenters on living cells, the investigations that he proposed to many of his students were carried out on fixed material. The explanation of this paradox lies in the fact that a great many of his experiments were made on sea urchins, a marine material. For this work he went to the zoological station at Naples, and only the fixed material returned to Würzburg for studies by the students. In the case of the roundworm, which formed the second major object of Boveri's study, the situation was similar although for different reasons.

In view of these circumstances it is worth noting that the program of the institute was not in the least influenced by Spemann's research, even though he worked there with live amphibian eggs for ten years, from 1898 to 1908, and was a close friend of Boveri. This was regrettable, for Spemann soon took a leading role in developmental physiology. The reason was that the number of biology students in Würzburg was quite small, in spite of Boveri's reputation. Most students who had a teaching career in view were attracted to Munich, the Bavarian capitol. Because of the small number of doctoral students in Würzburg, Boveri claimed them all for his own research area. He often complained, chiefly in letters to Spemann, about the scarcity of graduate students.

The small number of students in biology imposed limitations on the program of instruction for the first and middle semester of study. Most of the instruction lay in the hands of the single assistant provided in the budget of the institute. Here also can be seen Boveri's distaste for large-scale organization. Only in 1910 did he obtain from the Ministry a second assistant's post, which would have been granted him as a matter of course long before had he felt it justified and made the request.

It was not difficult to be the assistant in the institute at Würzburg. Boveri demanded little service and had no ambition for highly organized teaching. Furthermore, there was no pedantry in him. He tacitly expected from his assistants an intensive scientific commitment; steady, imperturbable habits of work won his confidence. At the same time, he provided for the fulfillment of his expectations, leaving the academic vacation, four to five months of the year, practically free for the student's own research. Since I was occupied with work on sea urchins and had to spend long periods in Naples, he even arranged generous furloughs, financed these also with a fellowship, and saw that there was a substitute assistant in the interval. He did not conceal that the instruction at the institute suffered from the substitution, but in his opinion the scientific training of a young investigator was more important. In his eyes, science and a scientific career were only in a limited sense a means of earning a living. Naturally, he conceded that the young scientist must live, but research must be, in the first instance, a true passion. It would have been pointless to think of an eight-hour day.

An episode from my own experience will show how unbureaucratic he was. As assistant, I had living quarters in the upper floor of the institute. There was a period when, a newcomer in my position, I did not come down to the laboratory until ten o'clock in the morning. Boveri came in at nine and very well might have felt that the assistant should be in the laboratory before the director's own arrival in the morning. He said nothing, however, for a long time. Then, on one occasion, he asked, "When do you usually get up?"

"Seven o'clock."

"Then what do you do until ten?"

"I work upstairs in my room, where it is quiet."

Then came his explanation that it was quite bad for the beginning of the day's work in the laboratory to have the assistant appear so late. The students took this for a sign to come late also. And his proposal was that it was quite all right to work upstairs, but that at intervals I should come down into the laboratory. This was very friendly and helpful. I understood the psychological background of his position only on reading Pauly's diary, which made it clear that Boveri felt himself restricted, as assistant to Hertwig in Munich, by prescribed hours of attendance. Thus in his own institute he tried to encourage freedom of time, primacy of research, and intensity of work. To illustrate his friendly relationship with the service staff of the institute, one can cite an accurate appraisal by the *Diener's* wife: "He certainly wasn't stuffy, our *Geheimrat*."

Another incident is characteristic of Boveri's indulgence for other individuals. If one were to compare the condition of the work tables in Boveri's laboratory with those in my room, one would be confronted with an unnerving difference. On his benches, spotless order; on mine, all surfaces covered with preparations, instruments, drawings, books. I felt I had a justified claim to more table space, and expressed this opinion to Boveri. I was turned down flat on the ironic ground that if I had another table it too would immediately be covered for all time, so that there would again be only a square foot of space left for me. His objection was completely right, and should have taught me something; but a sense of order appears to be an inborn trait in humans.

Unfortunately Boveri made no further remarks on the subject, and his decision did not reform me.

Let us now wander through the institute. The building consisted of three stories and was of imposing size for the time. That it was situated in a charming open area was no matter of indifference to Boveri. This space, the "glacis," was left after the leveling of the old fortifications of the town after 1866. In the garden of the institute a bit of the old city wall remained, and there was a pond left from the old moat.

The lowest floor of the building contained aquarium rooms and the living quarters of the *Diener* and his family. At that time this official was Bernhard Engelbrecht, who lived there with his excellent wife and two daughters. Engelbrecht, a former army sergeant, was laboratory factotum, and in addition collected a great share of the material for the elementary courses.

Following the German custom, Boveri offered an introductory lecture series four hours a week each semester. In the winter the lectures were on general zoology and invertebrates; in summer the subject was the comparative anatomy of vertebrates. The lectures were very close to his heart, and, at the same time, as he often admitted, were a burden that took too much time from his own research; yet he relinquished them to juniors only in periods of illness or during his longer sojourns in Naples. Financial considerations might have played a role, at least in his first years in Würzburg. But above all there was a moral obligation on his part to use the weight of his personality and experience in opening the biological field to the beginners, who were mostly young medical students. This he did admirably. He lectured without manuscript, quietly and tersely, not spectacularly. His reticent nature was not given to daily fireworks. The lectures nevertheless made a deep impression. When not drawing or demonstrating, he stood immobile behind the lecture table with his back to the blackboard, his eyes boring into the student audience, a picture of absolute concentration. The selection of material was extremely thoughtful; it was carefully limited to a few significant matters and formulated in the clearest possible words and drawings. Boveri said that he was continually simplifying his lectures. He seldom discussed fundamental questions as isolated abstractions; rather, he allied them to the presentation of significant animal types. Thus he used the slipper animalcule (*Paramaecium*) to illustrate the basic processes of living material, and *Hydra* for a discussion of germ cell formation. The student perceived this alternation of theory and fact as a harmonious and living whole. In particular, the first half of the winter course, comprising evolution, Protozoa, and cytology, was a masterpiece of pithy treatment. The comparative anatomy course, in which, contrary to tradition, he handled the different vertebrate types as unities, was a paragon of clarity. Considering his artistic gifts, it is not surprising that he was a master, at the blackboard, of clear schematic outline drawings with specific coloration, as well as of impressionistic sketches. At the end of the hour the blackboard would be harmoniously covered with colored drawings, as if an artist had distributed ornamentation on a screen. Here, as in many circumstances of daily life, he had the need of artistic form. His light hand would sketch some artistic object on the margin of a letter as freely as it wrote the address on the envelope.

Demonstrations followed the lectures. If these were drudgery, even despair, for the assistant, they were also proof of Boveri's predilection for living material, especially in the case of the Protozoa. He was not satisfied with the usual slipper animalcules and living amoebae; the elegant *Stentor* and *Vorticella*, *Volvox*, and budding and sexual forms of *Hydra* had to be shown living. Boveri insisted that they be set up with painstaking care and accompanied with explanatory texts and sketches. He was wretched when the assistant was unable to produce these types. Apparently it was his aesthetic pleasure in such beautiful forms that formed the basis of these demonstrations, which lasted scarcely a quarter of an hour and cost the assistant days of work. He would say, appeasingly, of this expense of time, "You may grumble at my pedantry, but the demonstrations are all I ask of you during the winter." This certainly was not the case, but in fact the painful process taught us that demonstration material should be taken, as far as possible, direct and alive from nature, not from books, and presented in a thorough manner.

Let us walk on through the first floor of the institute. There Boveri had his two laboratories, with a fine view of the trees of the glacis; regrettably, however, as we recall today his susceptibility to rheumatism, his rooms were almost without sun. In the seclusion of these two rooms his great works took form; we heard little, however, of their progress. The first drafts of dissertations were thoroughly discussed there, and it was always a moment of some anguish when one was called in for this purpose. One always found Boveri here before lectures, at the writing table sketching the figures with which he planned to cover the blackboard.

Not far from Boveri's rooms was the main laboratory of the floor, a long microscopy room with numerous windows, where the visiting scientists and the doctoral candidates worked. Each had the use of a large worktable that took up the whole width of a window. Individual places were flanked by small book and reagent shelves, so that each occupant was partly private in his niche, yet not separated from the general life of the laboratory. Here we students felt, in the fullest sense of the word, at home, partaking at the same time of an international life because of the presence of the foreign guests. The two groups were about equivalent in numbers: four or five doctoral candidates and an equal number of visiting research workers. The former, however, were the more permanent members. A dissertation with Boveri required some two years. The visitors often came for brief periods, expecting nevertheless to complete some project in this limited time. Boveri was capable of flying into a rage at such expectations. "They are perfect bloodsuckers," he wrote to Spemann, "and have departed with one or two 'completed papers.' I have now concluded to take nobody who will not stay at least a year."

In this laboratory Boveri appeared once or twice daily, walked from table to table, and asked each one if he had found anything new. If not, he went circumspectly on his way; he know how to wait. If one said yes, he would settle down at the student's table, as if he had unlimited time, to look at the new preparations and drawings. On these occasions his eyes became astonishingly, mercilessly sharp. His phrase was, "When I sit down at the microscope, I suspend belief." One had the feeling that he saw more in a few minutes than the student had perceived in hours or days. With similar precision he would compare the microscopic preparations with the drawings made from them. We had been taught by him that observation without drawing gives too little assurance; whole piles of sketches resulted. The common notion among students that only "publishable" cases were worth drawing withered and died at those worktables.

These visits often led to theoretical discussions. The thickset, seemingly ponderous man, almost motionless when speaking, would remain at the worktable of the student, leaning lightly on one of the bookshelves, his eyes fixed immovably on his companion. It was Boveri's eyes, of which the frontispiece in this book gives some idea, concerning which Wilhelm Wien the physicist wrote, "I shall never forget the penetrating, searching gaze, testing and piercing again and again, that was directed toward me when I came to Würzburg in the spring of 1900" (57:128). In spite of these eyes, Boveri was, in laboratory discussions, a sympathetic and encouraging companion, primarily interested in the thoughts of the student and keeping his own opinions out of the foreground. Under his direction, cytological work, precisely because of the fineness of the material, became a true education in rigorous critical observation and analysis.

After a student had accumulated a large quantity of observations and drawings in the course of one or two years, the time to write came. Daily visits ceased. Boveri did not care for the interim examinations or reports that are now usual. He waited until one presented him with a draft. In this second phase, the scientist in him was joined by the artist, who considered writing

LIFE AND PERSONALITY

from the standpoint of style. He therefore subjected the form of publication to criticism. Spemann, one of his first students, had experienced this. "My little first-born work," he wrote, "offered nothing essentially new. But by this not entirely easy investigation I learned microscopy; and by the writing I learned something more, scarcely less valuable to me. Boveri read over the first draft of my work and gave it back to me to rewrite, with the words 'You must now treat it as a work of art.' He was pleased with the second version" (1948:172).

What was impressive was that he actually took time for such textual criticism; only the students with a literary gift had their first drafts accepted without major correction, and usually one or several revisions were necessary. An indispensible requirement was, in addition to clear presentation of one's material, a clean distinction between facts and their theoretical significance. The reader, he insisted, must see without difficulty where the facts end and the interpretation of the author begins. We all know that even great scientists do not always follow this precept. When Boveri saw that a manuscript was not completely rewritten after such a judgement, but that pieces of the first draft were simply being rearranged, he put it down with an ironical, "Aha, you write your paper with paste and shears." Later, he amicably mitigated the irony of this remark by dedicating a copy of Schopenhauer's admirable essay "On Authorship and Style" to "F. Baltzer, for his edification and amusement." He often cited as an example the botanist Sachs, of whom it was told that he threw the first draft of his fundamental book on plant physiology in the fire, and wrote an entirely new second version.

The precision that Boveri demanded in drawing is not surprising in view of his exactness and his own graphic talent. I shall never forget his last words when he gave me back a cytological manuscript with many figures. "Do make," he said, "a final test to see whether drawings and text are in perfect agreement." He knew the danger of interpretations that were too optimistic.

Boveri founded only a small school in the direct line, although he attracted a large number of workers into his own field. Of the 24 doctoral candidates who studied with him during his 22 years of activity in Würzburg, only five continued an academic career. Deplorable as this was, the cause probably lay in great part in his own personality. As his works stand before us, rounded out in themselves, without rent or gap, so likewise his habits of work were isolated. He did almost all his work himself. A student, if he wished to take up a scientific career, was expected to find his own field of work. Boveri was very hesitant in advising a student to enter this career, even when the young man was not only scientifically capable, but in addition musical, so that Boveri would have particularly welcomed him to his circle. "I always dread a little to see one more soul embark on this sea," he wrote to Spemann, "when one does not know if there is land on the other side." This attitude bespoke a strong feeling of responsibility that he could not shake off. He would, in fact, have had more students if Munich, as the state capitol and center of modern culture, had not exercised a far greater magnetism than did Würzburg. In Munich Richard Hertwig had founded a large school.

It is obvious that students must eventually outgrow their master, that they will and must become independent. The higher the quality of the teacher the more difficult is this separation; not all teachers can take it with good grace. Boveri both sought to ease the separation of his students and to continue his advice when it was a question of an academic career. In a final criticism of the *Habilitationsschrift*, he declared that the relationship of teacher to pupil was at an end by saying, "This is the last occasion on which I feel entitled to exercise an influence."

Highly characteristic of both men is the description of the scientific development of Spemann in Boveri's institute, told in Spemann's autobiography. Spemann, at 25, was sent to Boveri by Pauly; the young man called on Boveri in Würzburg in the spring of 1894, and later wrote, "I had created for myself a fairly definite mental image of how he would look; my idea however bore little resemblance to the reality. He must have been aware of my discomfiture, since in our first conversation he remarked that people were always disappointed on seeing him for the first time. From his name they must have imagined an interesting Mediterranean figure." Spemann's description of Boveri's appearance follows, here somewhat abbreviated: "A medium-sized, thick-set, sturdy form of very upright bearing; a high forehead, built firmly and steeply as a fortress, all dominated by the eyes, which looked out, strikingly clear and tranquil, examining, steely, incorruptible" (1948:169).

The two men quickly became friends, as the letters show. Boveri found the Swabian easier to like than his North German colleague Wien, with whom he worked out a true friendship only slowly; the "Prussian language" and much of the North German manner was irritating to him.

Spemann took his doctorate in the following year, 1895, and was then looking for an experimental problem for his *Habilitation* thesis. "My strongest inclination," he says of himself, "was for a problem of general biological interest requiring technical invention. I asked Boveri if it would not be interesting to ascertain in what fashion the extraembryonic blood vessels take up yolk and carry it to the chick embryo." In fact, this question includes a significant and general problem of physiological or chemical embryology. Boveri was skeptical at first. "He did not believe," Spemann continues, "that anything new in principle would come out of it. Before beginning an investigation one should consider what can be expected from it. On the next day he changed his opinion. He had merely wished to say that one must always seek to attack questions the solutions of which will throw light over as great an area as possible. Perhaps the problem I proposed was of this sort."

In the end, Boveri suggested to Spemann another morphological topic for his *Habilitation* project. This concerned the development of the middle ear in Amphibia. One should, he said, once in one's life work on a problem of comparative anatomy. Here spoke the discoverer of the nephridia of *Amphioxus*. Only when the ear study was reaching completion did Spemann, by then 28, set out on his own course. In the interim he had begun the constriction experiments on the newt egg, which Boveri had followed day by day. It was Boveri's custom to go to Spemann's room after he had made the rounds in the general laboratory; we would hear them conversing.

In addition to this daily exchange of ideas, Boveri influenced Spemann's career in another manner when the latter was a candidate for the professorship in Rostock. The recommendation, requested of Boveri by the Rostock faculty, is significant for his careful judgement. The request was for an opinion on no fewer than nine young scientists; he placed Hesse, Spemann, and zur Strassen in the first rank. In a letter to the dean, in 1906, Boveri wrote:

> In this evaluation, which presumably differs materially from that of others, my principle is this: I prefer a man who sets himself a definite problem, the solution of which promises to deepen our general biological understanding, and who digs into it with all his powers. I should choose him rather than one who snatches one subject here, another there. From this point of view I place high value on the planned work of Hesse on light sensitive organs, and have even greater respect for the work of Spemann and zur Strassen in physiology of development. Spemann's *Habilitation* in Würzburg was ten years ago; at that time he solved a really difficult morphological question and had already begun to work in the field of developmental physiology in which he now holds an outstanding position. His performance has been marked by unusual acuity, very great technical ability, and an abundance of very exacting work.

Boveri then gives Spemann the preference over zur Strassen on the following consideration: "In zur Strassen's results, lucky accidents have played a much greater role than in Spemann's, which in my opinion promises better for the future of the latter." But even here Boveri maintained a balanced judgement, continuing, "I do not say he is better than all the rest, only that if the choice should fall on him it would be an excellent stroke on your part and I should congratulate your faculty sincerely." Spemann was called. He later became a Nobel laureate.

A final word of scientific characterization may be devoted to Boveri's summarizing lectures and addresses. A scientist remarkable for bringing together extensive series of facts into a unified theoretical frame must obviously have the aptitude for large-scale perspective. Boveri, however, was too little fond of publicity, writing, printing, even lecturing, to have composed many comprehensive reviews. In those days the means of travel for scientists were comparatively restricted and thus the opportunities for such lectures were much less frequent than they are today. As examples we may cite "On the Problem of Fertilization" (28), an address before the Society of German Natural Scientists and Physicians in 1902, and the famous paper "On the Constitution of the Chromatic Substance of the Nucleus" (32, 34), delivered in 1903 before the German Zoological Society. These addresses are distinguished by the same qualities as Boveri's great research reports. They approach the problem from many viewpoints, the theoretical discussion ranges broadly, the concepts are clear, and the judgements critical, both as regards original material and that of other authors. Moreover — especially significant in the case of lectures — the language is clear and graphic. A third major review, the Rectoral Address in Würzburg on "Organisms as Historical Beings" (42), will be more closely evaluated in the second part of this book in connection with Boveri's position on the problem of evolution.

Boveri's Memorial Address for Anton Dohrn (51),[6] delivered in 1910 at the International Zoological Congress in Graz, shortly after Anton Dohrn's death, requires special mention. It tells much about Boveri himself. In preparation he had gone to Naples for a few weeks, collecting biographical material and making use of notes that Dohrn had left.

[*] Quotations are from the text in the Congress Proceedings, with the exception of the one on the Marées frescoes, which is found only in the separate publication (on page 20).

The preliminaries in Graz were certainly not reassuring, as Boveri wrote to Röntgen. "Before the opening of the session, the President bowled me over with the words, 'I beg you, make it short.' As I assured him that it would take less than an hour, he replied, 'That is much too long. You can publish as much as you wish, but now make it as short as possible.' This was not very encouraging. However, I must say that there were expressions of gratitude from the audience." He had worked on the lecture for half a year.

Boveri had come to know Dohrn, 22 years his senior, quite intimately during his numerous stays at the Naples station; he was bound in friendship to Dohrn and to the station by personal experience. Hence the vividness with which the first sentences affected the listeners, many of whom knew the station at first hand. "Turn your thoughts to the dark green oaks of the Gulf of Naples, background of the beautiful white edifice with its red loggias, where the newly arrived zoologist, proud and happy, reads the inscription, "Stazione Zoologica," which tells him that this abode of science has been built for him and for his work too." And a later sentence also reveals Boveri's own experience. "How many prosperous investigations, how much joy of discovery, has this house known!" (51:280).

When Boveri first visited it in 1888, the station was a decade old. To recall the period of its founding, he sensitively brings us in front of the Pergola picture, the most personal of the now famous frescoes by Marées in the station library, "the document of that time, all the more valued as the time recedes. We see the friends sitting, at the end of the day's work, over a glass of wine in a ruined palace on Posillipo." Dohrn, somewhat depressed, is at the outer left; standing next to him is the zoologist Kleinenberg, chosen by Dohrn as head of the laboratory; next, the author Charles Grant, the interpreter of Neapolitan life and culture for the friends; and next to him Adolf Hildebrand the sculptor, "responsible for the architectural harmony of the station, only roughly sketched by Dohrn. Out of the background peers the painter himself who just then had created the frescoes that have made the station a place almost as much of artistic as of biological pilgrimage." In addition to the personal feeling for the enterprise and its realization, there is a deep sympathy with the personality of the founder, and this in spite of the almost total contrast in character, temperament, and way of life of the two men: Boveri the reserved, refusing to enter the whirlpool of scientific public life, accustomed to presenting his results with the utmost objectivity, when and only when they were complete, and living a settled daily life in Würzburg for two decades. In contrast, Dohrn was the man of immediate action, of stormy temperament, his activity arising out of a restless imagination, from a "passionate energy, even violence, in accomplishing what he felt right" (51:290); a man who had been tossed about Europe for a decade in dramatic controversies over his work.

If this memorial address enthralls by its intensity on a great subject, it is at the same time composed in a style of rare beauty and imagery, and with an emotion not to be found elsewhere in Boveri's writings, except in certain passages of the Rectoral Address. It bears witness to the artist that lived in Boveri side by side with the biologist.

Art, Nature, Friends

Boveri said of himself that he would have preferred to have become a painter; there are numerous drawings and oil paintings from his hand. His letters, also, contain many references to pictorial problems. This desire was, however, essentially a youthful dream. His artistic ability unquestionably was not nearly equal to his scientific gift.

It was no exaggeration, though, when he said that for him life without art would be wretched and scarcely worth living. His existence demanded surroundings stamped by art. Franconia offered him the fine old town of Bamberg, where he grew up, and Würzburg, where he worked. Würzburg was his home for over 20 years; this is reason enough for giving a picture of it here.

The town of Würzburg, grown to important size during the fifteen to seventeen hundreds under the reign of prince-bishops, lies in western Franconia on either side of the River Main, which flows through the countryside in a broad, ever-winding valley. Visible from far off, high over river and town, stands the Marienburg, a thirteenth-century fortress with walled ramparts. An old bridge adorned with picturesque baroque statues of saints leads to it over the river. Bridge, stream, and fortress together form one of the most beautiful views imaginable. This was the picture that Boveri often had before his eyes.

We have previously mentioned that the institute, together with other scientific and medical buildings, stood on the glacis, the promenade that had replaced the old ramparts around the town. Boveri's house was in the same area. At about nine o'clock in the morning he could be seen coming with measured step through the park on his way to the institute. Near his house rose the Steinberg, with its vineyards, the goal of many walks, offering a fine view of the River Main and the town.

Within the glacis began the ancient town with its many angled streets and alleys. Along these stood numerous picturesque old town houses; saints adorned the house fronts. In contrast to these narrow streets, two large market places formed a spacious center for the town, where the country people congregated on market days. The center was dominated by church buildings of earlier centuries. Not far away was the Residence of the prince-bishops, one of the finest German baroque palaces of the eighteenth century, with a large public garden and magnificent forged-iron lattice gates.

Every man, in addition to the space of his daily life, inhabits a much wider territory of the spirit, compounded of past and present. In this spiritual world, Boveri lived with music, architecture, and the fine arts. Among buildings, he admired especially the Cathedral of Bamberg, in the shadow of which he had grown up, with its great Roman forms and the figures at its portals.

In the realm of painting and drawing, he valued especially,

among the old German masters, Grünewald as a colorist and Dürer as an engraver and draftsman. In contemporary painting, Würzburg offered little. Since Boveri had to take part in examinations in Munich every year, he had the opportunity of visiting exhibitions and modern collections there. He especially liked Hans Thoma and Karl Haider for their deep sympathy with nature, Leibl for his fine painting and accurate representation. "Leibl holds his own," he wrote after a visit to the museum at Cologne where there were numerous Leibls, "in competition with the finest old Netherlanders," which he and his wife had seen in Holland. By contrast, the symbolic art of a Klinger did not appeal to him.

Through Pauly, as early as 1887, he had met Karl Haider, who at that time was struggling to make a reputation. In order to help him as far as his slender means would permit, Boveri bought a drawing, the sketch of an Apostle with his head pensively supported by his hand. "Boveri," noted Pauly, "got a good thing there — almost frighteningly good, since it is one of the best drawings Haider has made. If it were 300 years old one would call it a jewel and pay heaps of money for it." Boveri remained in contact with Haider and later acquired a self-portrait of his.

It is natural that as a frequent visitor to Naples Boveri should be strongly captivated by Italian art, and also by the history of the fourteenth and fifteenth centuries. Jakob Burckhardt's *Culture of the Renaissance* was one of his favorite books. On his study wall hung large pictures of the Castel Sant'Angelo and the Roman Forum. In the large Italian museums, to be sure, he was disturbed by the tourist industry since he required tranquility and silence for contemplation of art works. There is a humerous reference in a letter to Wien (57:142): "I stopped overnight in Milan and thought of paying a call on Madame Gioconda who was likewise visiting there." The famous Leonardo from the Louvre was temporarily being exhibited in Milan. "But what I heard about the conditions of this interview impelled me rather to go to Florence to admire other less courted beauties in peace.

I was again completely overpowered by Michelangelo's figures in San Lorenzo."

Würzburg had another charm for anyone living there any length of time. Franconia had been ruled by prince-bishops up to the period of secularization of church property in Napoleonic times. The many old towns were in Boveri's day still rich in good, old handicraft products, particularly in ecclesiastical objects. Würzburg was a central market where it was still possible to buy good Gothic woodcarving. Boveri had a very lively interest in these minor arts. Below are reproduced extracts from an exchange of letters with his sister-in-law in Baden, showing how enthusiastic Boveri could be in such commerce. The letters are a mixture of fancier's delight, eagerness to buy, artistic appreciation, and humor.

Boveri was commissioned by his sister-in-law to buy one or more old wood figures for his brother. Confronted by especially attractive offers, he could not restrict himself to a modest deal. Thus, somewhat terrified, he wrote to his sister-in-law (November 24, 1909): "Before reading this, I beg you to take a chair. Yesterday I bought some old wood figures for two thousand marks. It was a case of closing immediately or letting the chance slip. There are 14 figures, not for sale singly. All originate from the same altar, and a major part of the value lies in their correlation. It was a difficult decision for me, and cost me a pretty sleepless night; I have once more sworn never again to go shopping for others. Naturally, as you can judge from the price, the figures are not masterpieces, but they are very good Gothic work, defective in various respects but by the same token not botched by later repair. The old paint is there, where not peeled off, enriched by the dirt of centuries." Then two weeks later: "I must write you again about your saints. The figures have in the meantime been inspected by both our art authorities. The head of the art museum fell in love with one of the large figures: without doubt the best piece, finest work, relatively the best preserved painting, has something very charming that grows on one. The museum

LIFE AND PERSONALITY

has a similar one, he says, but ours is definitely better. He wanted to take it with him for 600 marks. As I said that was much too little, he admitted, 'Well, it is worth a thousand, but I have to make bargains.' He said the lot is a very good buy."

Finally, he writes, on December 16, "The saints departed today by express." And as the last word, "In addition to these figures one more is coming; I call it 'Bode's wood bust.'[7] It interested me so much that I got it on approval. Dr. Pinder, who is at present making a study of Franconian sculpture of this period (ca. 1490) saw it at our house, fell into ecstasies, could at first not place it, and finally decided that the head is thirteenth century and very like certain figures on the Bamberg Cathedral."

Among poets Boveri was especially fond of Gottfried Keller, whose works fascinated him by their artistry and vividness of narrative, even more by their humor and originality; but perhaps also because of the melancholy latent in them. Like Keller, Boveri combined outward restraint with a volcanic temperament. He was particularly familiar with *Green Henry*, no doubt because he would have liked to be a painter. He also took special pleasure in the comic situations in *The People of Seldwyla* and delighted in teasing the younger people in the laboratory about the three righteous comb makers and the maiden Bünzlin. Even at the institute he was always ready with humor and good-natured mockery. These were the elixir of life to him, compensating for his emotional restraints.

Boveri enjoyed reading — often in company with his wife — biographies and correspondence of important artists, such as the letters of Clara Schumann, which struck a responsive chord by their empathy with Brahms' music in preference to Wagner's. He similarly enjoyed the correspondence between Brahms and Joachim and between Brahms and the Herzogenbergs. As for painters' lives and art theory, he was attracted by the memoirs of Hans Thoma, "where there are many fine things," and by

---

[7] Wilhelm Bode was at that time director of the Kaiser Friedrich Museum in Berlin.

Cornelius' *Elementary Principles of Fine Art*. He was also concerned to share these interests with his younger colleagues. The present author, together with Gerhardt Kautzsch, who was a member of the Würzburg Institute during 1910, was often a guest at the Boveri home. There we regularly found and enjoyed selected books on plastic or graphic art spread out for us on the living room table.

Music, however, was sovereign. Boveri was a very good pianist. When he came home from the laboratory he regularly sat down at the piano. For him, playing was at once a release from science and an entrance into the world of the muses. Much four-handed music was played in that house, sometimes on one piano, sometimes on two pianos. Kautzsch was a welcome partner. At the Boveri home, in a period when radio and gramophone were still unknown, one received a broad education in musical literature. This ranged from classical concerti grossi and symphonies to the chamber and symphonic music of Johannes Brahms. Boveri's performance at the piano showed two characteristic qualities, namely great rhythmic precision and the ability to comprehend at first sight the essentials of a score.

Personal sympathies developed most easily, even in Boveri's later years, in musical companionship; this was true, for example, of his friendship with the philosopher Külpe in Würzburg. Although music could act as a real intermediary in relationships with his young colleagues, he consciously excluded such sympathies when forced to form an objective judgement. He once wrote concerning a young man whom he would have liked as assistant but whose scientific initiative he mistrusted, "A pity; he is such a nice fellow and plays piano so well that I would be glad to keep him here."

It was consistent with Boveri's character that Bach should stand very high with him. A friend once remarked that one might hear a fugue from the Well Tempered Clavier or a Beethoven sonata played with more virtuosity, but hardly with deeper expression than Boveri gave it. He was able to unite personal interpretation with attentive subordination to the purposes of the composer. To see him playing Mozart four-handed with his little daughter made an unforgettable impression; not surprisingly the child had to be extremely alert to satisfy her father. He was, moreover, well aware of his technical limitations and, when he played alone, preferred compositions over which he had complete mastery. He was far from being a genius who outruns his own powers.

For this artistically many-sided man who had wished in his youth to be a painter, it is clear that the brush had maintained its claim. The only one of his oil paintings which survived the war bombing is a landscape of the Bavarian foothills, painted around 1908. The realistic, careful manner explains his admiration for Thoma and Haider, although he once remarked that Haider might just as well have used a rubber stamp for his trees.

Boveri did not set high value on his own painting and showed his pictures only to close friends. But he nevertheless said of himself, with reason, that he was happiest as a painter; this activity offered him most fully an undisturbed and intimate dialogue with nature.

The Boveris had inherited from the maternal side a well-appointed country house in Höfen, half an hour from Bamberg. The *Seehaus*, formerly church property, lay in the midst of broad flat meadows with fine groups of trees and a fishpond. This house played an important role in Boveri's life as a place of rest and retirement. A guest there could observe to Boveri's love of nature in its fullness. As a schoolboy in the '60's he had caught the likeness of the house in a delicate pencil sketch; later, in his role of careful custodian of tradition, he wrote a brief chronicle on the subject, the first lines of which may serve as a sample of his handwriting (page 48). According to this account, the house was built in 1711 by the resident prince-bishop of Bamberg as a fishing retreat; it was surrounded by large fish pools. "According to family legend," reported Boveri's chronicle, "the ecclesiastical lords came out from Bamberg occasionally for the fishing as well as for fish dinners. A few pieces of furniture in the dining hall (in the upper story of the house) stem, according to family tradition, from the time of ecclesiastic reign. The greater part of the fish ponds were later changed into pasture land and the house itself was enlarged in 1903."

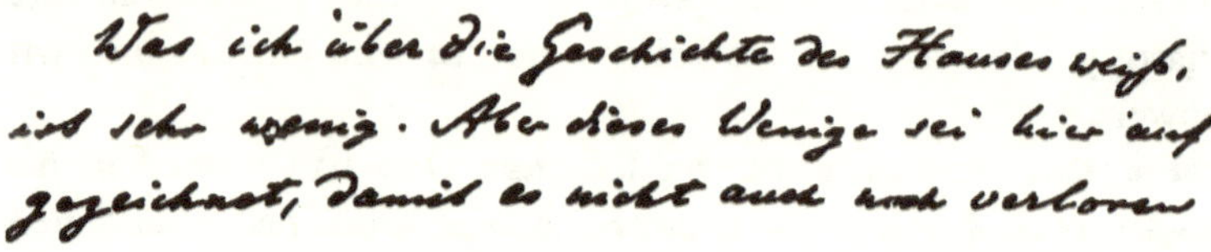

[handwritten German text]

First lines of Theodor Boveri's chronicle of the *Seehaus* at Höfen. Approximately two-thirds of original size.

In addition to this refuge in the delightful Franconian countryside, easily reached from Würzburg, Boveri had in his youth an especially favored holiday place in the mountains. It was a primitive woodcutters' inn in the Alps of the Chiemgau on the Förchensee, a mountain lake which one of his friends described as lying "like the eye on a peacock's feather, between steep rock walls and dark firs." There a small circle of friends gathered, led by Pauly and the painter Haider. Shared feeling for the magnitude and silence of this landscape, earnest discussions, minor scientific observations, and all manner of merry jokes, turn by turn, held the friends together. "There Boveri's whole personality, his deep feeling and his humour, came to the surface along with the ability that his mother had observed in him to put work aside at the right moment and to give himself to joy" (57:124). In spite of the Alpine surroundings, Boveri did not become a mountaineer. When Pauly tried to convert him to leather shorts and hobnailed boots, because, as he claimed, "this way one gets over dangerous places more safely," Boveri drily replied, "Where *I* get to, it isn't dangerous."

Later, when Boveri was physically unequal to the primitive life at the Förchensee, and perhaps also to oblige his wife, the family spent holidays farther south and more comfortably. He

LIFE AND PERSONALITY

visited his brother Walter in the Engadine, where he enraptured nephews and nieces with romantically colored impromptu sketches on a great slate table at the inn. On such occasions he had, besides unfailing humor, the gift of making amusing verses.

Anyone who has been in the Engadine and Bergell knows how cold it can be on the heights of the Maloja Pass, and how warm at the same time it can be in nearby Bergell. He perhaps also knows the bewitching village of Soglio there, with its inn in the fine old Salis palace and its view over the crystalline mountains of the Bondasca. To this village Boveri dedicated the following strophes (57:136) on a postcard to Wien, then in Mittenwald in the Karwendel mountains:

> When in the Oberengadine,
> One can, when breezes blow too keen,
> Pack boxes, bags, portfolio,
> And drop to Bergell, to Soglio,
> Where, from mild and temperate wealds
> The eye seeks out the glacier fields,
> The wondrous peaks, the lonely crags,
> Complete with dentate zigs and zags,
> To which your overprized Karwendel
> Cannot pretend to hold a kendel.

In Cadenabbia on Lake Como, for many years the Boveris joined the Röntgens and other friends "for a quiet stay, without being hounded to walk." Röntgen was especially close to Boveri. "We agree," the latter wrote in the year 1910, looking back, "in many things, and in the almost 17 years we have known one another, we have lived through much together. We both like a quiet life, when possible in beautiful natural surroundings, with a few intimate friends with whom one may talk or be quiet as one wishes." In addition, however, to this southern holiday resort, the homely Höfen remained a beloved retreat. On this subject Boveri wrote an affectionate strophe, again to Wien, in August, 1909 (57:135–136):

> Wherefore strive for distant treasure
> When the best lies close around?
> Hell with the Alps: we take our pleasure
> Here on Grandma's meadow ground.
> Days are sunny, nights are breezy,
> Duty sleeps, the grub is good;
> Tired virtue now can take it easy
> In the shadow of the wood.

николаиNAPLES

The first pages of Boveri's memorial address for Anton Dohrn, the founder of the zoological station at Naples, show how much Naples meant to Boveri himself. The station was a marine research laboratory and a meeting ground for biologists. In those days it was imposingly situated on the beach in a beautiful park at the edge of Naples. The Gulf of Naples also appealed to him as a center of antique art, Mediterranean landscape, and southern way of life.

Boveri first worked in Naples during the winter of 1887–1888; then during two spring months in the years 1889, 1894, 1896, again in the winter of 1901–1902, during the spring seasons in 1905, 1910–1912, and finally in the winter of 1914. Work in Naples thus traces through Boveri's life like a recurrent theme with variations. For him these sojourns always meant renewed liberation in the full sense of the word; on occasion, recalling the fruitful times spent in Naples, he referred to his whole activity in Würzburg as a "miserable existence." However great the exaggeration, he certainly was able, as soon as he got to Naples, to leave university business and instruction behind him and to devote himself freely to research. Also, from 1900 on, his wife collaborated on his projects. In all, about 20 of Boveri's studies originated in the Naples Zoological Station, and when in the Dohrn memorial address he spoke of how much joy of discovery the station had witnessed, he spoke for himself.

We shall attempt, on the basis of letters written from Naples by Boveri to his friends, especially to Pauly, Spemann, and Röntgen, to create a picture of his days at Naples. Unlike the usual visitor to Italy, he went there in the often unpleasant early spring season. The ground for choosing this time was simple and decisive. All his work there required sea urchin eggs; this material is in best supply during the colder months. The beginning of the summer semester, with resumed teaching, set an often unwelcome time limit.

Boveri was 25 years old when at the end of 1887 he made his first trip to Naples. He described it in a long letter to Pauly on January 14, 1888, giving a lively and, as Boveri enjoyed doing, rather drastic and unfairly generalized sketch:

> After I left you that Wednesday evening, I bought a bottle of the wine you recommended, a great sausage, and half a loaf of bread, on which I lived all the way to Naples, with the addition of some cups of coffee. In Ala, at the frontier, on my first encounter with an Italian waiter, I had the opportunity to observe the shameless manner in which these scoundrels try to cheat foreigners. In change from a fifty-lire note the fellow calmly gave me three lire too few and went off with the most innocent expression. When I noticed the shortage, I first thought it would be too late to reclaim. However, I called him back and counted out the money to him. He then, without a word, laid the missing three lire on the table.
>
> Thursday morning, in beautiful weather, we had a splendid crossing of the Alps, warm and free of snow. For one just out of the German snow, it was like a fine spring day. Unhappily the snow returned before Modena; in Bologna it was deeper than at home. The flat country in Lombardy makes a sad impression. It was bitterly cold in the unheated carriage. At Bologna we at least got large hotwater bottles for our feet.
>
> From here on I travelled in exclusively Italian company and thus discovered the virtuosity and sheer delight with which the Italian expectorates. A fellow sat beside me who, every two or three minutes, sprayed the opposite wall in a long sizzling stream; he aimed and hit every time within quite a small area and each new charge landed just a little above the last. Since I have been smoking the miserable Italian cigars, I quite understand how this talent can be developed.

Of Florence I saw (it was already night) only the station promenade, which makes a very dignified impression, really suited to prepare one for the treasures lying concealed in the city. Perhaps the night had a share in evoking the impression in me.

Early Friday at seven o'clock we entered Rome. I took advantage of the one-and-a-half hour stopover to walk about the town a bit. What I saw was ordinary modern. Only here and there ruins grey with age jut out among houses and gardens. It was truly more the *thought* of the place where I stood than the sight of it that transported me to a solemn mood. Here I saw for the first time the type of elegant priest — not unpleasing. The trip from Rome to Naples, again in the finest weather, was wonderful. Here the Italian character of the landscape, of which Victor Hehn[*] is able to impart some preconception, struck me with full force. I considered how a painter must profit from a journey to Italy. I believe the key lies in the *newness* of the form and color that here suddenly meet the eye. This difference from the accustomed must certainly shock a painter out of his habitual and lifelong mode, reinforced by stereotyped depictions, of observing nature. What we at home experience as shadow, distance, and so on, expresses itself here as color. It is somewhat similar when we look through our legs at our landscape, only that the orientation is not lost. Here I believe one can learn, provided one is capable of learning, to see the individual object according to its essential nature.

One's first view of Naples is Vesuvius. I believe it was in the vicinity of Capua that a very blasé Italian, who had not vouchsafed one glance at the beauties of the passing scenery during the whole journey, indicated the window and with great importance pronounced the word "Vesuvio," as if to say, "Try to match that if you can!" It is a special sensation when one finally sees with one's own eyes something of which one has read and heard so much: cypresses and pines, orange and lemon trees covered with fruit, palms out of doors, the Italian in his natural surroundings.

I later learned that Davidoff was at the railroad station to meet me; we missed one another however. You cannot possibly picture to yourself the life that reigns in the streets of Naples. One con-

---

[*] The reference is to Victor Hehn, *Italien, Ansichten und Streiflichter* (Berlin). Several editions were published in the 1880's.

tinually expects to be run over. The noise as first is absolutely stupefying. The cabmen and vendors recognize every foreigner from afar and fall upon him. One cabbie drove along beside me for some five minutes, screaming to me in French that he would drive me anywhere I wanted.

After I had rid myself of the accumulated dirt of several days' travel, I took an afternoon walk, precisely the most beautiful walk one can take here, right along the sea. On the way I saw the zoological station, for the time being only from the outside. It lies close to the sea, surrounded by the handsomest public garden of Naples, the so-called Villa Nazionale. Here there are concerts three times a week, and the whole of elegant society can be viewed. The women are, as a whole, by no means attractive; the exceptions are all the more charming. I have unfortunately not yet had more intimate experience. The tarts do not walk the streets; instead, one is laid hold of, evenings, by men who recommend "jolies dames" to one. This is scarcely to my taste, buying a pig in a poke.

When I think of all I have to write about the eight days I have spent here — the city, the environs, the station, the museum, theater, lodgings, company, and so on — I am so at a loss that at the moment I had rather not begin, preferring to close with the assurance that I feel extraordinarily well. As soon as I am a bit more in the groove I shall write more properly. In the museum are two splendid Titians, the only pictures that I have really looked at there so far. Tomorrow I shall probably go to Pompeii.

In this first stay, Boveri was lucky in the matter of weather, and also with his material, which formed the basis of the third *Cell Study*. Moreover, he had the opportunity for free-and-easy association with numerous colleagues. Ten of them lived in the same *pensione* as he, and they ate together; among these was August Weismann, whose views were soon to lead them into lively discussions. With the Neapolitan population, of whose shortcomings he was acutely aware, Boveri never made a positive adaptation. He was unable to disregard the annoyance of importunate beggars and unreliable cab drivers. More than once, on a carriage drive interrupted by a broken wheel, he reacted by flying into a rage at the carelessness of the coachman and the unforeseen delay in the outing. He diffused his ire not only on the wretched cabbie but also on the young companion of the trip, who sympathetically paid the official charge. "He even paid him, the ass!"[9]

The second visit in the spring of 1889 was by contrast "somewhat troubled." Snow fell. The weather was very stormy and there were corresponding difficulties with the sea urchin material. Furthermore, Boveri felt overworked and was suffering from colds "in the present beastly weather." The company, also, he found not so attractive. For his work, however, the period was very important. In this spring he first carried through his famous hybrid merogony experiment, which will be discussed in detail in the second part of this book. To Pauly he wrote, "A comfort in this weather is the splendid library. I have especially been looking more closely into the old papers of v. Baer, Johannes Müller, and others, an invigorating occupation. What a contrast to the dozens of volumes that are inflicted on us here each week. Moreover, I have read a couple of plays of Ibsen that seem to me pathological indeed, but which read far better than they play on the stage. I expect to move on from here in a fortnight or so to spend another eight to ten days prowling about Italy."

The difficult merogony experiment was repeated in 1896 in collaboration with McFarland, with variable results. "We have in general the most filthy weather imaginable, to which I am accustomed from earlier years. One freezes, and there is no place where one can be comfortable. Now and then there are exquisite days, however. I have made several expeditions, and am in good humor, although the experimental results leave much to be desired. We are tormenting ourselves precisely with the isolation and fertilization of enucleated egg fragments. No one but my fellow-sufferer and myself can form an idea of the agony involved." Such experiments "can bring one almost to despair," he wrote to Spemann.

[9] It may be of interest, however, to note that, on a similar occasion in his later years, it was Boveri who preached *pazienza* to other outraged foreign visitors.

The subsquent visit, during the winter of 1901-1902, was especially fruitful, showing how rapidly and intensively Boveri could work. He had, for the first time, the "constant, expert assistance" of his wife. On the way to Naples he had stopped for a time in Villefranche. There he discovered, in the egg of *Paracentrotus*, the characteristic equatorial ring of red pigment. He recognized that this made it possible to ascertain how much the animal and the vegetative portion of the sea urchin egg could each perform in embryonic development, a decisive point in the discussion with Driesch (see pp. 110-114). "I now believe," he wrote to Spemann from Naples on December 1, 1901, after only a month's work, "that I can with full confidence assert the inequipotentiality of the sea urchin egg."

At the same time he began the classic experiments on double fertilization of the sea urchin egg that led him to the proof of the diverse value of the chromosomes. In the same letter to Spemann, Boveri wrote, "It now appears to me beyond doubt that the individual chromosomes must possess different [hereditary] qualities, and that only definite combinations permit normal development."

As Boveri often recounted, he and his wife worked at that time in the large laboratory of the station which also accommodated Driesch and Herbst. He later enjoyed recalling this stimulating association. At Herbst's suggestion he had adopted the former's new method of separating cleavage blastomeres by means of calcium-free sea water, a procedure he at once recognized as extremely favorable for his experimental purpose. With Driesch also there was a particular connection. The mortality in doubly fertilized sea urchin eggs had been observed independently by both men (43).

The Boveris also lived in the same *pensione* as the other two investigators. "At the table we sit," he wrote to Spemann, "next to Driesch and Herbst. There have been many weighty discussions, in spite of my wife's veto, since these sessions have a bad effect on my night's rest. The strength and weakness of Driesch have become even more apparent to me."

Despite rapid progress, the investigations on the development of doubly fertilized eggs were not completed until the next stay in Naples, in the spring of 1905. At that time too the experiments went well. "It is remarkable how, under identical working conditions, the intervening three years have simply been, as it were, effaced."

Among the other visits may be mentioned only the last ones of 1911-1912 and 1914. He felt his age. "For me Naples is a very good measuring instrument of aging — not an agreeable experience." However, he accepted this patiently and permitted himself relaxations. "Since my box [his instruments] had not yet arrived, I went off to Capri the next day, where I spent five precious days with marvelous weather and an almost complete absence of other foreigners. Day before yesterday I settled again into my old room, and so I am slowly relearning to work." In these last sojourns, the problem was again the hybridization of enucleated egg fragments. "It is, as I have known for a long time, the most prickly experiment one can attempt with the sea urchin; but I feel under obligation to settle this matter once and for all." The decisive results, which will be discussed in the second section (see pp. 82, 83), were not, however, obtained until 1914 and were accepted with painful resignation. Boveri had to recognize that his earlier method of enucleating the eggs by shaking did not yield reliable material.

Epilogue

> Alterius non sit, qui suus esse potest.
> PARACELSUS

Let us attempt, before considering Boveri's work in detail, to bring together the striking traits of his personality.

The letters of Boveri himself and the testimony of the friends of his early years show us a sharp and critical observer of his surroundings, and at the same time a man with an independent inner life. The basis of his character may be outlined in the following terms: strong moral force in critical situations; an unshirking sense of responsibility, inflexible love of truth; an inner sense of order, placing first things first; and freedom of judgement.

He had the ambition to be a great scientist and he was conscious of his accomplishment without failing to realize the endlessness of scientific problems. He despised every form of limelight and had no desire to concern himself with external aspects of the scientific world. Vanity did not touch him. Finding it in famous colleagues, he would comment ironically.

Illness followed him from his early years. When in bad health he was tormented by doubts concerning his creative ability. On this subject we learn more in retrospect from his letters than could have been gathered while he lived. When he said that he could live only at the upper limit of his physical capacity, this conviction arose from the extraordinary intensity of his mode of work as well as from very high scientific standards and limited bodily strength.

In later years Boveri appeared externally cool and composed. His emotional nature seemed repressed. But the richness of his personality remained and, beneath the composure, so did the old, sometimes unexpectedly rough and irritable temperament. A compensation lay in his alert, imaginative, and drastic humor.

Family and friends were familiar with the emotional side of his character. He was a very sympathetic father, and to his friends a true and constant companion. Always ready with a helpful act, he was at once strong and sensitive. Towards us, his juniors by a generation, when he felt a rapport he behaved with watchful friendship. Moreover, the all-embracing nature of his insight, to which nothing human was alien, permitted him to be fair even to unsympathetic characters. For his younger colleagues, his personal example and the manner in which we saw him live and work made an unforgettable impression.

He lived at a time when public and private life began to suffer from pressures and overstrain. But in spite of a heavy load of work and duties, he maintained the inner strength to find quiet and repose. He found them in many places — in the depths of scientific thought, in the work of great artists, in his daily life with those near to him, and in the world of nature around him.

In 1915, after Boveri's untimely death, E. B. Wilson wrote a commemorative article (57:67 ff.) that was both impressive and objective, extracts from which we shall use to conclude Part One. The two men had become acquainted when Wilson came to Munich in 1892 to work with Boveri. From that period they remained close personal and scientific friends with similar research interests. Wilson by 1918 was the leading cytologist of the United States and had dedicated to his friend his book *The Cell in Development and Heredity*, a work of admirable comprehensiveness. In the commemorative article, Wilson wrote:

> The work of Theodor Boveri, not less than his life, recalls to mind the saying of the ancient Scriptures that man does not live by bread alone. For, as the interests of his life reached far beyond the limits of the laboratory — he was, for instance, a skilled amateur of painting and of music — so his work was remarkable not alone for what he did but also in the manner of his doing. That work was in high degree original, logical, accurate, thorough. It enriched biological science with some of the most interesting discoveries and fruitful new conceptions of our time. But beyond all this it is distinguished by a fine quality of constructive imagination, by a sureness of grasp and an elegance of demonstration, that make it almost as much a work of art as of science. In this respect, as I think, Boveri stood without a rival among the biologists of his generation, and his writings will long endure as classical models of conception, execution and exposition.

PART TWO:
SCIENTIFIC WORK

Almost the whole of Boveri's scientific work, as he himself once said, was devoted to the *investigation of those processes "by means of which, from the parental reproductive materials, a new individual with definite qualities arises* (50:133). The basic problem of his work was thus, in the broadest sense, that of heredity and development. This includes three research fields: cytology, since the egg and sperm are cells: embryology, since the definite qualities become visible only as the egg develops into an embryo; and finally, genetics, since the genes of the germ cells, in collaboration with the cytoplasm, determine the expression of these definite qualities. It was the triumph of the period to which Boveri belonged that the findings of these three fields came to be united into a conceptual whole; and precisely here, Boveri's theoretical views, far transcending his own data, were of pioneering significance.

As cytologist and embryologist he was a master of microscopic methods, endowed with extraordinarily sharp eyes and accustomed to mercilessly critical analysis. He was, at the same time, an outstanding designer of biological experiments. Watchful and respectful, not to say reverent, in regard to the living object, he sought to intervene in the mechanism of the developing egg and embryo. Over all stood a keen, speculative spirit seeking the great problems and correlations without thereby losing sight of the facts. In Boveri's work, observation, reflection, and experimental result were united in a rare harmony.

Among his investigations, we shall first describe the chromosome studies, which are concerned with nuclear division and the nucleus as carrier of heredity. From these studies three important theories emerged: the concept of the individuality of the chromosomes; the centrosome theory of fertilization; and the theory of the differential (genetic) value of the individual chromosomes. Next are the investigations on the egg cytoplasm and the relations between it and the chromatin. Finally we shall discuss the comparative anatomical studies on *Amphioxus* and the Rectoral Address on "Organisms as Historical Beings."

INTRODUCTION

When Boveri began his scientific career in 1885, cytology was already an imposing edifice. It was known that organs and tissues in all multicellular organisms were composed of elementary units, that is, cells, and that each of these units was composed of

---

FIGURE 1. Mitotic nuclear and cell division. First cleavage of the sea urchin egg. Semi-schematic, from stained preparations. Original. *a*. Egg cell with interphase nucleus showing "diffuse" chromatin network. Adjoining the nucleus, the duplicated centrosome (C) with astral radiations. *b*. Nucleus in prophase. Individualized chromosomes form from the chromatin net (16 chromosomes arbitrarily shown). Nuclear membrane disappearing. Radiation spheres appear around centrosomes. *c*. Mitosis in equatorial plate stage (metaphase). The original chromosomes lie in the equatorial plane and have divided into daughter chromosomes. *d*. Anaphase stage. The asters and the daughter chromosomes have pulled apart. *e*. Telophase. The daughter chromosomes become vesicular. The equatorial cytoplasm between the asters begins to constrict. The centrosomes have divided again. *f*. Reconstruction of the daughter nuclei. The chromosomal vesicles unite into a single nucleus. The centrosomes produce new radiations in the cytoplasm. Cytoplasm nearly divided in two. *g*. and *h*. The mitotic cycle of the second cleavage begins in the daughter cells (blastomeres).

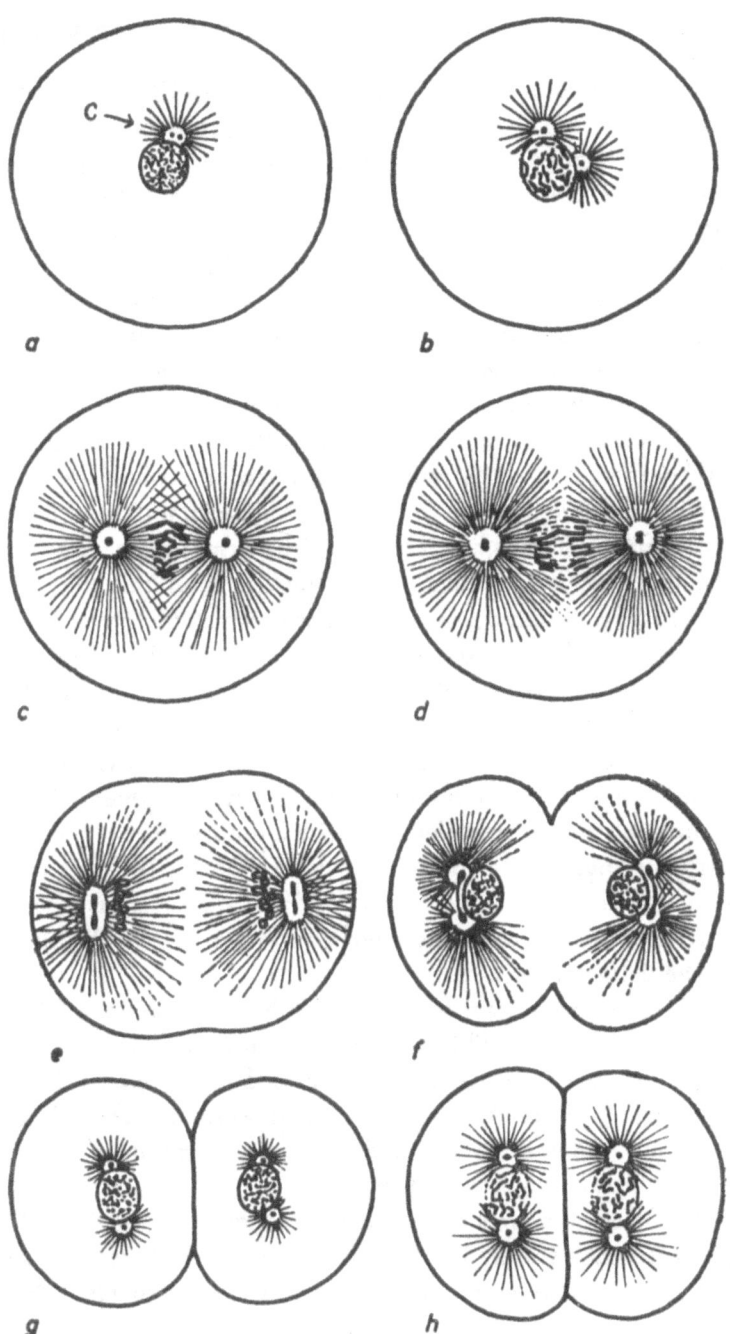

a protoplasmic cell body containing a vesicle, the nucleus. It was also known that cells in animals and plants multiply by divisions, which go hand in hand with corresponding divisions of the nucleus. It is by such cell divisions that the egg after fertilization becomes a many-celled embryo. It was also established that nuclear division (karyokinesis) proceeds similarly in all organisms. From the vesicular nucleus (fig. 1*a* and *b*), small individualized rods or loops appear — the chromosomes (fig. 1*c*), of definite form and constant number for each species. At the same time, in the plasma outside the nucleus, two centers of radiating fibrils are formed. Slightly later, as Flemming had established (1880, 1881, 1882), the rods or loops appear doubled by longitudinal splitting. From the mother chomosomes then, double the number of daughter chromosomes arise. In the meantime, the two radiating centers have united to form the poles of a spindle (fig. 1*c* and *d*), in the equator of which the chromosomes are aligned. Next, the daughter chromosomes, as E. van Beneden (1883) showed, are equally distributed to the two spindle poles. Thus to each of the daughter cells, which then assume spherical form, one about each pole, is allotted an equal chromosome assortment. Finally, the chromosomes in the two daughter cells are formed into vesicular nuclei, each with a similar diffuse chromatin network (fig. 1*f*). In the subsequent and later cell divisions the same pattern of events is repeated. From the vesicular nucleus, chromosomes again appear, double, and are equally distributed to the daughter cells.

These processes occur in all forms of life in so similar a fashion that it seemed plausible to consider them universal. Equally important, a concrete foundation seemed to be offered for the understanding of inheritance. Egg and sperm are cells, though strikingly different in size and form; each contains a nucleus, from which chromosomes develop.

A first advance was made when the botanist Naegeli, in 1884, proposed theoretically an "idioplasm," a specific hereditary substance including within its fine structure the individual "vital formula." In the same and in the following year, several men — van Beneden, Strasburger, Oskar Hertwig, v. Kölliker, and Weismann — almost simultaneously arrived at the conclusion that Naegeli's idioplasm must lie in the chromosome substance. Nuclear division and chromosomes became the center of a distinct field of biological investigation. Richard Hertwig, the brother of the aforementioned Oskar, deserves the credit for directing Boveri to this field. Boveri acknowledged this advice with gratitude on several occasions, although he had struck off on his own path immediately after entering Richard Hertwig's laboratory.

The Belgian embryologist E. van Beneden (1883) had discovered extraordinarily favorable research material, the egg of *Ascaris megalocephala*, the parasitic threadworm of the horse. The nucleus of this egg forms only four chromosomes; in one especially favorable race only two chromosomes are present. The small number of chromosomes, in addition to their relatively large size, permits the processes of nuclear division to be followed with especial ease. These advantages decided Boveri's choice of material. He started working on *Ascaris*, and there appeared, with one year's interval, the two first large *Cell Studies*, devoted to this object.

The first of these studies (6) is concerned with the maturation of the *Ascaris* egg. "On the one hand I was seized by the desire," the author says, "to observe with my own eyes the fundamental facts of fertilization in van Beneden's object; on the other hand, it seemed to me that the formation of the polar bodies, as shown by this investigator, required independent verification" (6:429). Each maturing egg, by means of two "maturation divisions," gives off half of its nuclear substance in two "polar bodies," and thus reduces its chromosome set by half. The eliminated portion is replaced by the sperm chromosomes as a result of fertilization.

In the same year (1887), Weismann advanced the theory that in maturation a new combination of chromosomes is brought about, and thus brings a shuffling of hereditary material. This prophetic suggestion lacked confirmation by microscopic analysis; Boveri could not supply this by his observations on maturation in *Ascaris*. Nevertheless, his studies formed a substantial foundation for further work. It speaks for the scrupulousness and high precision of Boveri's observation that his figures of the maturing *Ascaris* egg have to this day not been superseded and still have their place in cytological texts.

I. THE CHROMOSOME STUDIES

The Theory of the Individuality of the Chromosomes

Without a break in the continuity of the work, the second *Cell Study* followed the first one by one year (8). Far more extensive than the first paper, this one is devoted to the fundamental problems of chromosomes, showing the author's mature mastery in his field. In addition to a multitude of new important facts, the study shows great theoretical power. Before representing his own work, Boveri testifies to his great admiration for van Beneden, 16 years his senior, in words that make it clear which scientific qualities he himself most valued. "Though van Beneden has enriched our insight into the life of cells by a series of *fundamentally new facts*, equally imporatnt in my eyes is his astonishing *intellectual penetration into the material*: the way and the means by which he considers each seemingly insignificant detail, combining one with another; the way in which he illuminates each observation from all sides, pursues each in all directions, and thus is able to derive a new concept from each phenomenon. The book contains a plenitude of questions and ideas, and I gladly acknowledge how much stimulation and instruction I have derived directly from these qualities in it" (8:688). These were the qualities to be found also in Boveri's own work.

The second *Cell Study* placed Boveri in the first rank of cytologists. Its great contributions lie in the advancement and sharp formulation of the theory of chromosome individuality and the proofs given for it; the presentation of the centrosome theory of fertilization; and the analysis of the relation between chromatic and achromatic processes.

If the chromosomes are hereditary substance, they must have

continuity, since in continuity lies the essence of heredity. But it was exactly this property that seemed to be lacking in the chromosomes. In the vesicular interphase of the nucleus they were not demonstrable in Boveri's time. The conjecture that the chromosomes, even when they disappear into a diffuse nuclear network, still retain their identity as persistent elements, had already been voiced by van Beneden (1883) for *Ascaris* and, independently, by Heuser (1884) for nuclear divisions in plant cells. Then Rabl, in a penetrating work published in 1885, was able to show that the chromosomes of epidermal cells of the salamander larva appear in a similar radiating position *before and after* each interphase. This seemed to be an argument for an arrangement persisting in the diffuse chromatin network. Boveri added the decisive information that in the mitoses of the *Ascaris* egg the same chromosome arrangement may be found before and after the interphase. However different one case may be from another, the same arrangement recurs regularly in paired daughter cells. "When, regularly, in both cleavage cells," he says (8:838), "almost the same relative position of the four loops is found, this can be explained only by their derivation from a common source," that is, *from the chromosome arrangement in the mother cell*. Since *Ascaris* has only four or, in the race univalens, only two chromosomes, the proof was much more clearly obtained than in the salamander cell with 24 elements. In figures 2a and b and the

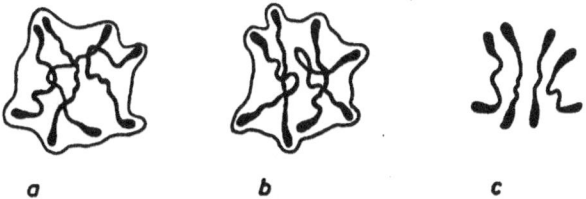

FIGURE 2. *Ascaris megalocephala*, roundworm of the horse. Bivalens race with four chromosomes. *a* and *b*. Nuclei of early two-celled stage (prophase). The chromosomes lie symmetrically in the two daughter nuclei (cytoplasm not drawn). *c*. Schema of the chromosome positions in 2a and b. From Boveri (8), Figure 83 *a–c*.

scheme 2c an example is shown. Identification of the elements is facilitated by the peculiarity that in *Ascaris* the ends of the chromosomes tend to remain in individual outpouchings of the nuclear membrane.

In the second *Cell Study* the number of completely unquestionable cases was still limited. Nuclei can rotate in the cytoplasm, making it difficult to ascertain the relative position of chromosomes. It is a sign of great perspicacity that Boveri nevertheless formulated his and Rabl's findings in the clearcut hypothesis of the "individuality of the chromosomes" and claimed general validity for it, even going so far as to say that the chromosomes were "autonomous individuals that retained this autonomy even in the resting nucleus" (8:689). With similar audacity he defined his position, with regard to physico-chemical concepts, that the cell is not "a simple composite of chemicals" as would be the case if it were "only a question of very intricate chemical and physical processes." Again, the ultimate components of the cell that we can recognize as distinct, formed elements are also *organized* structures, which "as units in their manifestations of living processes, defy interpretation through physico-chemical forces" (8:692).

Although many facts spoke for the individuality theory, objections were expressed, and among the objectors were to be found "the very powerful voices" of O. Hertwig and of R. Fick. With Fick an embittered discussion began, lasting into the first decade of this century, which we shall review briefly, since it is instructive not only for the character of both scientists but also for the history of cytology. It shows how long the individuality concept, formulated in the '80's, provoked an opposition that scarcely seems credible today. According to Fick's view (1899, 1905, 1907), the chromosomes were merely constellations of maneuver, temporarily formed for the regular distribution of the chromatin, and thoroughly mixed and altered in the next interphase nucleus. The reader will comprehend that this view completely denies any significance of the chromosomes as individual bearers of heredity. Fick published two detailed critiques in 1905 and 1907. Boveri, thus attacked, replied in 1909 (46). In the meantime he had found very well preserved material of the race *Ascaris megalocephala* univalens, which has only two chromosomes. Here much clearer cases of chromosome arrangements were easy to find as compared with the previous bivalens material where four chromosomes were present. Figure 3 gives an example. The legend may be consulted for details.

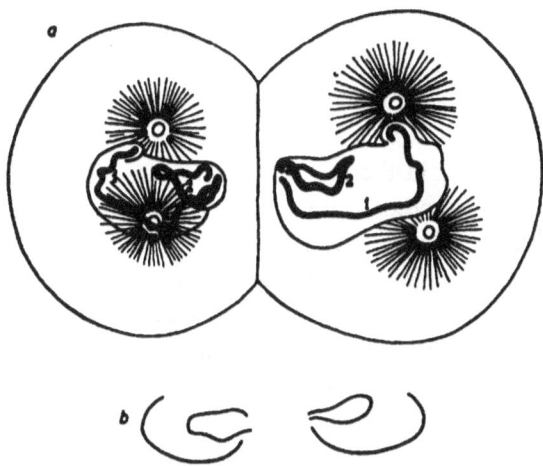

FIGURE 3. *Ascaris megalocephala*. Univalens race with two chromosomes. *a*. Egg in two-celled stage, nuclei in prophase. The chromosome loops in the two nuclei lie in almost corresponding positions. Their deeper-lying portions are shown by shading. Cell bodies with spindles and asters also shown. ($\times$ 2,000). *b*. The position of the chromosomes shown schematically. From Boveri (46), Figure 24.

The 1909 paper shows Boveri as a vehement, inflexible, and relentless assailant, who this time is determined to crush his opponent to earth. It also shows his conceptual sharpness, advancing the claim that the value of a theory must be judged exclusively according to the facts, and that in its critical evaluation "light and shadow must be scrupulously assigned." In Fick's article, however, as Boveri expressed it, we have to do with "a partisan tract," with an "uttermost negativism," with a "tendency to destroy. The carefully assembled building blocks, with which others seek to construct a substantial lofty edifice — admittedly incomplete at present — he reduces to a heap of rubble. When the most important members supporting the theory are shoved aside, when, before foundations are laid, the upper blocks are placed free in the air, obviously they will not stand, and it is easy to cry with Fick, 'See, they are falling down,' " (46:264). On no other occasion did Boveri indulge in such vehement polemics. However, in this discussion he also argued the concept of chromosome individuality more closely (43, 46), and freed it from a certain rigidity found in his earlier publications. It is not a question, he specified, of a permanent identity in the mathematical sense. He conceded that an individual chromosome could alter chemically without losing its individuality.

Fick (1909) recognized after this reply the strength of evidence offered by the new material, and might with justice have claimed for himself the merit of having instigated this publication of Boveri's — an attribution undoubtedly not acceptable to his opponent.

Since those days, a half-century of research has passed over the theory of chromosome individuality. It was basically, as Boveri conceived it, a *morphological* idea. For him, the chromosomes were really structured, "organized elements existing autonomously in the cell" (34:9), which as such are passed from one cell generation to the next, and from one individual to its offspring. He also used the expression "symbiont"; in fact, since then, the genes or hereditary units which in large numbers occupy the chromosomes have been compared to symbiotic viruses. The basic perception of Boveri, that the chromosomes despite their simple outward form are highly organized structures, was later strikingly confirmed, *inter alia*, in the chromosome maps of *Drosophila*. Boveri's first morphological conception, however, had to give way to more elastic formulations. In this sense, Wilson wrote in 1925 (p. 828) that chromosomes could no longer be pictured as fixed unalterable bodies. "What the facts do not permit us to doubt is that the chromosomes conform to a principle of genetic continuity; that every chromosome which issues from a nucleus has some kind of direct connection with a corresponding chromosome that has previously entered that nucleus." In this elastic formulation Boveri's morphological view retains its validity today. The investigation of the fine structure of chromosomes has become a chemical problem. But the principal component of the chromosome, deoxyribonucleic acid, preserves its individual macromolecular "morphology" over the generations and reproduces itself in nuclear division according to its own structural pattern.

Boveri's Theory of Fertilization

In addition to the individuality theory, a large portion of the second *Cell Study* was devoted to the events of fertilization. Here also, Boveri presented a basic new theory. Let us briefly recall (following Boveri's own discussion) the development of this problem, old as mankind. It has always been understood that father and mother contribute about equally to the characteristics transmitted to the offspring. What was difficult to understand was how the father could exert such an influence. The year 1875 brought a decisive advance. "At that time," writes Boveri (16:394), "all conditions requisite for a complete penetration into the problem had been, by degrees, fulfilled." Egg and spermatozoon (the latter had been discovered by Leeuwenhoek and Ham in seminal fluid 200 years before) were known to be cells. The microscope had already reached the state of technical perfection required for a thorough analysis and, last but not least, a technique was evolved enabling the investigator to render visible cell organelles that had previously eluded all observation. Nevertheless, attempts to discover the true relationship in the events of procreation had not been successful. "It was thus the uncontested merit of Oskar Hertwig to have, with a single brilliant stroke, illuminated the field. Up to that time, relatively unsuitable material had been used for study:

large opaque eggs such as that of the frog, or eggs fertilized internally and therefore practically excluded from observation at the critical time. O. Hertwig [1875] selected for his first investigation the eggs of a sea urchin (*Paracentrotus lividus*) and found thereby an object in which so many favorable circumstances coincide, that even today — at least for observation in the living state — it is unsurpassed" (16:394). It has been a frequent experience in biology that the discovery of a suitable object of study may open access to a great new field of investigation, and even today, nearly a hundred years after Oskar Hertwig's discovery, the sea urchin egg is one of those most frequently used for such studies. Boveri himself used this material for a very important part of his investigations. The eggs are transparent, small (about 1/10 mm in diameter) and accessible for examination with high magnification. In the living state, the mature egg shows an evenly granular cytoplasm and a pale vesicular nucleus (see fig. 12a). The sperm cell, by contrast, is extraordinarily small (fig. 4a); it has an anterior thicker part, the so-called head, only 1/1000 mm in length, which contains little besides the compact, condensed cell nucleus. To this is joined a tiny knob, the middle piece, to which in turn is attached the movable tail fiber, the vibrations of which keep the sperm cell in continual random motion.

If one takes eggs lying in sea water and adds an extremely small amount of the milky seminal fluid that flows from the testis of the male animal, the sperm cells can be seen after a few instants collected in great numbers around the eggs. The heads are so oriented as to unite with the egg surface. "But only one sperm reaches this goal, the one that first touches the naked egg surface. Now the less reactive egg also shows a tendency for union. It extends toward the sperm a little hillock which surrounds the head and middle piece and thus takes it into the interior of the egg protoplasm" (28:7) (fig. 4b). This union of two extremely unlike cells is the beginning of the new individual. Some five to ten minutes after the addition of sperm there appears, quite near the egg surface, a small homogeneous body, the sperm nucleus,

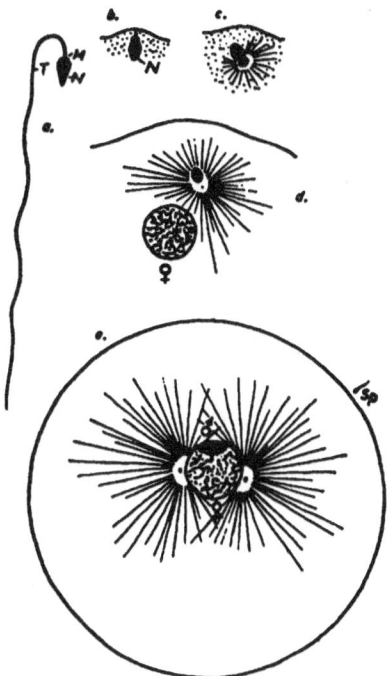

FIGURE 4. Fertilization of the sea urchin egg. *a.* Sperm cell: N, nucleus; M, midpiece; T. tail. *b.* Sperm nucleus and midpiece, just after entrance into the egg cytoplasm (stippled). The tail remains outside the egg. *c.* Formation of an aster around the midpiece. *d* and *e.* Approach of the sperm nucleus to the egg nucleus (♀) and union of the two nuclei (♂ ♀). In *e*, Sp shows a sperm cell at about the same magnification as the egg ($\times$ 500). Figure 4*a* after Harvey (1956), Figure 11; *b–e* from Wilson (1925), figures 184 and 185.

which, suitably treated, stains bright red with carmine as does the egg nucleus (fig. 4*b* and *c*). It moves, surrounded by astral radiations, toward the egg nucleus (fig. 4*d*), with which it unites (fig. 4*e*). In this way the first cleavage nucleus is formed, the division of which will initiate embryonic development.

From these observations Oskar Hertwig concluded that the essence of fertilization, after copulation of the sperm and egg cells, lay in "the union of two sexually different cell nuclei, the egg and sperm nuclei." For a long time, Hertwig, under the impression of his classical observations on the sea urchin egg, considered the union of nuclei to be the sole decisive factor. But as early as 1883, van Beneden showed that in the *Ascaris* egg this union is omitted and the parental chromosomes enter directly into the first cleavage spindle, an omission that Boveri in his third *Cell Study* (12) confirmed for other animals as well. These observations directed attention away from the nucleus as a whole and toward the chromosomes within it.

FIGURE 5. Fertilization in the worm *Sagitta*. All 9 chromosomes of both sperm and egg nuclei visible. Nuclei not fusing. From Boveri (12), Figure 19.

At the same time Boveri was able to show for various marine forms that from sperm and egg nucleus arose two similar chromosome arrays. As a striking example, egg and sperm nuclei of *Sagitta* are shown (fig. 5). This was an insight of great significance. Certainly the two sex cells differ extraordinarily with regard to cytoplasm: the egg a nonmotile, often yolk-filled cell, rich in cytoplasm; the sperm, extremely motile by means of its flagellum, but almost without cytoplasm. In chromosome content, however, the two cells are equal. Thus, assuming that the chromosomes contain the hereditary material, it could be understood how father and mother are equally important in transmitting characteristics to the offspring. On this basis, the doctrine of chromosome individuality would assume great importance. If chromosomes retain

SCIENTIFIC WORK

their individuality from division to division, it follows that in embryonic development all cells of the body, which have arisen from the fertilized egg, possess a chromosome array half maternal, half paternal. Each cell must then contain an equivalent quantity of hereditary material from each parent.

Let us now turn to the middle piece, a second, very small component of the sperm (fig. 4a–c). O. Hertwig had not observed it originally. Impressed with the behavior of the nuclei in fertilization, he had not dealt with the question of how exactly the egg is stimulated to further development. Van Beneden (1887) and Boveri (8) however had observed, in the center of the astral rays of the dividing *Ascaris* egg, rounded granules which divided when new asters were formed. Both observers interpreted these as the *formative centers* of the radiations, and the radiations as the means by which the chromosomes were distributed to the daughter cells. Then Boveri posed the question of the origin of these centrosomes or formative centers. A penetrating analysis of the sea urchin egg showed that in fertilization the middle piece is taken into the egg along with the sperm nucleus (fig. 4b). In the middle piece is a centrosome which by division forms the two centrosomes of the cleavage spindle, of which all centrosomes of the later body cells are descendants. Boveri's theory of fertilization thus included two parts. The event decisive for *heredity* is the combination and reproduction of a maternal and a corresponding paternal chromosome set containing the hereditary substance. The decisive event for *development* of the egg is the introduction of a specialized organ of cell division, the sperm centrosome. This replaces the aged and no longer functional egg centrosome.

This automatically raises the question of how this organ of cell division cooperates with the nucleus. Two cyclical processes are involved. In the cytoplasm, the regularly repeated division of the centrosome is accompanied by the formation of new radiation spheres, the activity of which causes cell division. On the other hand, the chromosomal and nuclear cycle alternate just as regularly.

The "achromatic" and the "chromatic" processes are ingeniously correlated in normal cell and nuclear division. Boveri devoted a large part of the second *Cell Study* to their interplay, and in later work returned to this "dualism of mitotic phenomena" (8:870). Both processes are largely autonomous. The centrosome in a cell devoid of nucleus and chromosomes can divide and form asters; likewise, chromosomes can divide into daughter chromosomes independent of a centrosomal division. In only one phase, namely when the centrospheres have become united in a spindle, are the two processes coordinated. At that time, the dividing chromosomes are actively arranged by the spindle fibers in the equator between the two poles. The daughter chromosomes are equally distributed to the two spheres and thus to the two daughter cells (fig. 1c and d).

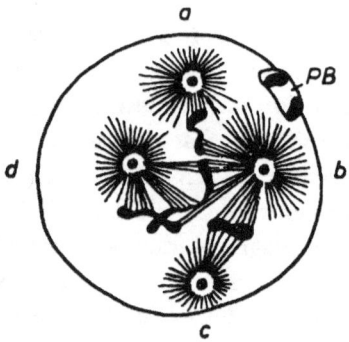

FIGURE 6. Tetrapolar spindle in an egg of *Ascaris megalocephala* bivalens. Chromosomes arranged on several spindles. Of the four poles, two (a and c) will receive only one chromosome, b will receive three or four, d, two. PB, polar body. From Boveri (8), Figure 93.

Boveri showed that in this duality "the karyokinetic processes are adapted solely for a binary division of the nucleus" (8:869). By contrast, multipolar division figures, which occasionally occur in normal *Ascaris* material, almost invariably lead to abnormal conditions. Such cases had been subjected to critical analysis in the second *Cell Study*. Boveri was fond of such exceptional cases presented to him by nature. "Almost every abnormal figure, insofar as it excludes one or another of the many, often multiple, possibilities admitted as originally causing and conditioning a phenomenon, must promote our insight and strengthen our judgment" (8:871).

An example of such an instructive anomaly is reproduced in figure 6. "What is most striking about it," says Boveri, "is that each chromatic element is related to only two poles, although no explanation of this can be found in the disposition of the centrosomes and chromatin loops. It is evidently not always the nearest central body whose fibrils attach to a loop" (8:852). It followed from such cases that the chromosomes are bilaterally constructed, and that any one loop can be attached to not more than two centrosomes. This principle of chromosome structure has proved to be generally valid. When more than two centrosomes with their radiating spheres are present, it is a matter of chance to which poles the chromosomes will be distributed.

We shall return to these findings in the discussion of diminution in *Ascaris* and again in the discussion of dispermic sea urchin eggs, on which material Boveri, in 1901, carried through one of his most important experiments.

Let us briefly return to Boveri's theory of fertilization. Its two parts have not proved to be of the same general validity. The principle of combination of the biparental chromosome sets has remained valid up to the present day. On the other hand, Boveri had later to restrict the significance of the sperm centrosome as a fertilization organ. In various ways it has been possible to stimulate the egg to develop in the absence of a sperm centrosome. The most famous case was that of the sea urchin itself. Jacques Loeb, in 1899, was able to replace the fertilizing activity of the sperm by chemical factors (butyric acid and sea water of increased salt content) and thus to stimulate the egg to "chemical parthenogenesis." Furthermore, botanists showed that in higher plants no centrosome at all is present. Wilson (1925) points out, however, that none of these considerations alters Boveri's conclusions concerning normal fertilization in *Ascaris* and similar forms.

The Nucleus as Carrier of Heredity, Experiments on the Sea Urchin Egg, Merogonic Hybrids

Cytology, from the time of its inception in the year 1839 until the 1880's, developed chiefly as a descriptive science. It then turned increasingly to experimental methods, and this change is mirrored in Boveri's work. What we have reported of his work in the preceding pages characterizes him as a descriptive microscopist. The proposition that the union of the egg and sperm nuclei in fertilization brings together two similar chromosome sets was likewise the result of pure observation. However, observation alone could not settle the question whether these morphologically similar biparental chromosome arrays were developmentally equivalent in the offspring. *Experimental* verification was necessary.

In the spring of 1889, during his second residence at the Naples station, Boveri performed two different experiments on the sea urchin egg. One of these experiments will be dealt with very briefly here, the other more extensively.

In 1887, O. and R. Hertwig had shown that it is possible, by shaking, to break sea urchin eggs into pieces which can be fertilized by sperm of the same species in the same manner as total eggs, and thus be made to undergo development. Many of these fragments contain the egg nucleus, visible as a small vesicle; others are without a nucleus. Even these egg fragments devoid of an egg nucleus can develop if they are fertilized (fig. 7d), and can indeed, as Boveri showed, form completely normal larvae (10). This demonstrates that the paternal chromosomes alone, in collaboration with the egg cytoplasm, suffice for normal development at least up to a specific larval stage (pluteus). In this case, a paternal-haploid larva was formed. In figure 7b and e two larvae are shown. One was raised from a *nucleated*, the other from an *anucleate*, equally large egg fragment, both fertilized. In the latter case, as well, a normal larva has developed with typical gut and skeleton.

The complement to this development with the paternal nucleus

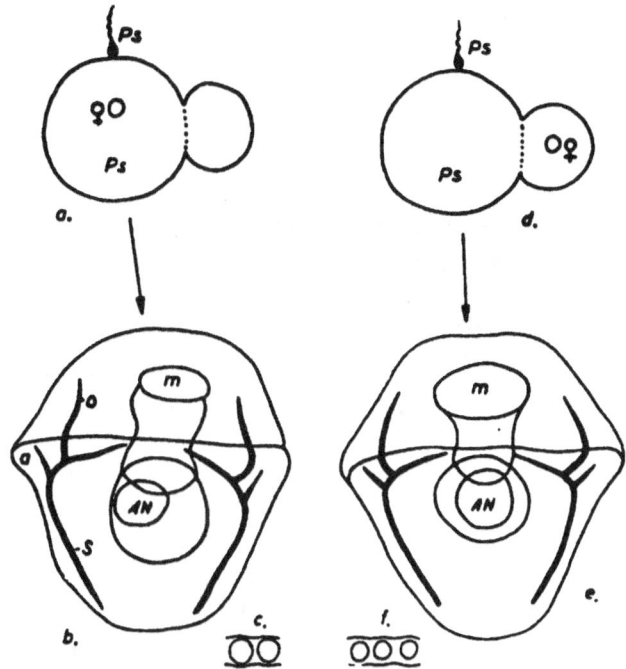

FIGURE 7. Development of fragments of the sea urchin egg (*Psammechinus*), fertilized by sperm of the same species, to normal pluteus larvae. *a.* Fertilization of an egg fragment containing the egg nucleus (♀). *b.* Young pluteus developing from 7a. Its nuclei have both maternal and paternal chromosome sets (diploid condition). *c.* Diploid nuclei from 7b. *d.* Fertilization of an egg fragment lacking nucleus. *e.* Young pluteus, from 7d, containing only paternal chromosome set in its nuclei (haploid condition). *f.* Haploid nuclei of 7e, same magnification as in 7c. Ps, *Psammechinus* cytoplasm or sperm. AN, anus. M, mouth. Skeleton: a, anal rod; o, oral rod; s, apical rod. The dotted lines in *a* and *d* show schematically where the egg fragments have broken away from one another. Figures 7a, b, d, and e drawn from life; c and f from fixed and stained material. From Boveri (40), figures 1 and 2.

is furnished by maternal-haploid eggs which develop with only the chromosomes of the egg nucleus. Boveri found such eggs as an exception; normal larvae develop from them. A more elegant proof was offered later by the chemically parthenogenetic sea urchin eggs in experiments by Loeb (1899). It was shown, therefore, that the chromosome sets of egg nucleus and sperm nucleus, morphologically alike, are also, with certain reservations, developmentally and genetically equivalent.

In addition to these general results, the culture of haploid sea urchin eggs gave impetus to further investigation in two directions. It was demonstrated that in animal development in general, there are definite relations between chromosome number, nuclear size, and cell size (the nucleo-cytoplasmic ratio of Richard Hertwig). In sea urchin development in particular, chromosome number, nuclear area, and cell size are directly proportional. Thus one can determine by the size of the nucleus how many chromosomes it contains. Boveri, in 1905, devoted his fifth *Cell Study* (40), from which fig. 7 is taken, to this relationship.

Furthermore, numerous cases in which the haploid state arises under natural conditions, could now be interpreted. As is well known, in the honey bee the drones develop from unfertilized eggs and have a haploid constitution. In other invertebrate groups, too (aphids, cladocera, rotifers), parthenogenetic generations provide rapid multiplication in summer. The haploid chromosome set furnishes the complete inheritance. The lack of fertilization and of the male sex simplifies reproduction. In the plant kingdom there are large groups in which the constitution is haploid.

The second experiment, again on the sea urchin egg, follows directly from the Hertwigs' and from Boveri's own discoveries. It has become famous as "merogonic hybridization."[10] It also marked the beginning of a long road of frustration for its originator. For although Boveri sacrificed more energy and time to this experiment than to any other (10, 21, 30, 53), it ended 25 years later in failure (56).

The general problem was as follows: all findings up to this

[10] *Meros* is Greek for "part." In this experiment fragments of shaken eggs were fertilized.

point had agreed in showing that the nucleus plays a major role as hereditary substance. However, the counter-question had to be posed: What role does the cytoplasm play in reference to the nucleus? Does the much more bulky cell body influence the type of the developing embryo, or has the nucleus absolute primacy and is the cytoplasm merely building material?

With the knowledge that egg fragments lacking the egg nucleus can be fertilized and can develop into normal larvae, a new possibility was indicated. Boveri now essayed to fertilize such anucleate merogonic fragments with the sperm of a different species having a characteristically different larva. The development of such a hybrid merogon, if development did occur, would give decisive information. If the embryos showed only characters of the paternal species, brought in by the sperm, the nucleus must be the sole bearer of heredity. However, if characters of the maternal species appeared as well, then cytoplasmic influence must also be operative.

A test appeared possible if anucleate egg fragments of *Sphaerechinus* could be fertilized with the sperm of *Psammechinus* or *Paracentrotus*.[11] The pluteus of the paternal species is shaped like a pointed cone. There is a simple calcareous skeleton; in particular, the anal arms are composed of single rods (fig. 8a). *Sphaerechinus* plutei, by contrast, have a blunt cone shape and, instead of the simple anal rods, a "lattice rod" composed of three longitudinal elements connected by cross bridges (fig. 8b). Normal hybrids, in which both maternal and paternal nuclear material is present, are intermediate in skeleton and in outer form (fig. 8c). There is no lattice rod, but with occasional exceptions the anal rod is not simple but is composed of two or three parallel rods without cross bridges. The merogonic cross should be decisive: if the nucleus is the sole bearer of these characters, then an anucleate

[11] In the following account, only *Psammechinus* is referred to as the paternal parent. Actually, in about an equal number of experiments, not *Psammechinus* but *Paracentrotus* was used as the donor of sperm. It might be noted that *Psammechinus* was previously called *Echinus*, and was so designated by Boveri, whereas *Paracentrotus* was at that time called *Strongylocentrotus*.

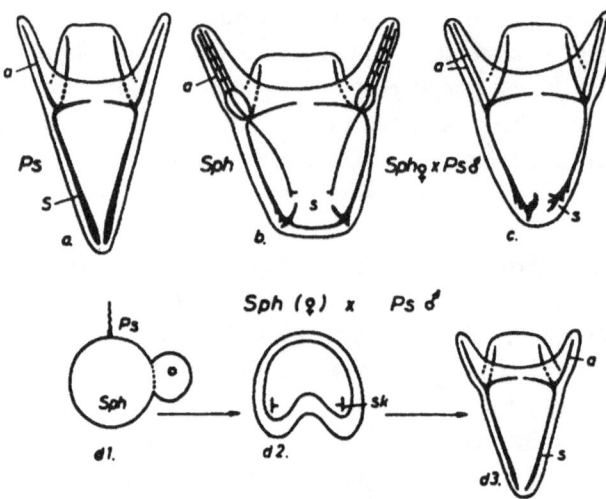

FIGURE 8. Larval types (pluteus) of the sea urchins *Psammechinus* and *Sphaerechinus* and their hybrid. *Paracentrotus* closely resembles *Psammechinus*. *a. Psammechinus* larva (Ps). Skeleton with simple anal rods (a) and club-shaped apical rods (s). *b. Sphaerechinus* larva (Sph). Skeleton with latticed anal rods and branched apical ones (s). Later the apical branches will close to form a quadrangular frame. *c.* Diploid hybrid pluteus *Sphaerechinus* ♀ × *Psammechinus* ♂ with intermediate skeleton: usually two parallel anal rods without crosspieces; apical rods branched. *d* (1–3). Development of the merogonic hybrid *Sphaerechinus* cytoplasm × *Psammechinus* sperm. *d*1: fertilization of an anucleate *Sphaerechinus* egg fragment. *d*2: inhibited gastrula (almost all embryos of this combination die in this stage; Sk, rudiment of skeleton). *d*3: hybrid merogone of the same combination with purely paternal skeleton. All plutei drawn in anal view from life. From Boveri.

egg fragment of *Sphaerechinus*, fertilized by a *Psammechinus* sperm, should develop into a pluteus with purely *Psammechinus* characters. If, however, the cytoplasm is involved in inheritance of these traits, some *Sphaerechinus* qualities must be seen.

This was brilliantly thought out, but much more easily conceived than performed. The hybridizations succeed only in a small proportion of cases. One can imagine with what excitement the experimenter approached the decisive test. Large quantities of *Sphaerechinus* eggs were shaken, then *Psammechinus* sperm added. Occasional eggs remained intact after shaking. These developed into typical intermediate hybrid larvae. Many smaller larvae showed identical characters. These were hybrids from egg fragments containing the egg nucleus. "Another portion of the dwarf larvae, however, corresponded fully to the paternal larval type. They must obviously have developed from anucleate fragments. There remains," concluded Boveri (10:78), "no other interpretation than to trace the dwarf larvae of purely paternal type . . . back to the nonnucleated egg fragments" (fig. 8d_3).

Nevertheless, these mass-cultures had a serious drawback. Boveri could "easily obtain many millions of eggs and egg fragments" and the large number of fragments could compensate for the small number of successful hybrid fertilizations. But in mass-cultures he could not follow the development of any single merogonic embryo. To settle this uncertainty, he had attempted, as early as 1889, a more direct method. From the shaken material, he selected single nonnucleated fragments, in all about 200, and tried fertilizing these with *Psammechinus* sperm. "I did not have the luck," he concluded with resignation, "to see one of them develop" (10:79). This in itself is not surprising, since successful fertilization can be expected in only about one out of a thousand eggs in this combination.

If Boveri had to be satisfied with mass-cultures, another improvement could be made. "One can observe, on a fixed and stained larva, whether it developed from a nucleate or a nonnucleate egg, precisely by the size of its nuclei," and he found that in the dwarf larvae with purely *Psammechinus* characters the nuclei were "always considerably smaller." His interpretation thus seemed certain. He wrote that "practically every doubt has been eliminated and the proposition that the nucleus is the sole bearer of heredity has been confirmed. When the maternal nucleus is absent, the inheritance of maternal characters is likewise eliminated" (10:80).

In the matter of nuclear size, however, Boveri was pursued by unusual bad luck. The nuclei of the larvae classed as hybrid merogons in the 1889 material were in fact smaller than those of normal plutei. He fixed these dwarf larvae, stained their nuclei, and sealed them in glycerin in order to measure the nuclei more critically later. When he got to them after some months, "all important preparations had lost both their calcareous skeletons and the nuclear stain, through acidity of the glycerin. In my first discouragement," he added, "I prematurely threw them out" (40:446). The possibility of making a thorough study of nuclear size in this material was thus lost.

Boveri had published the 1889 results in the summer of the same year. The report aroused great attention, but in various directions came up against contradictions which Boveri himself had to recognize. It was a weakness in the argument that the isolated fragments had not been successfully cultured; in 1895 another such attempt failed. He also had to admit that in occasional cases, hybrid eggs *with* egg nucleus developed into paternal-type plutei. "Nevertheless I believed," he wrote 25 years later, "that I could hope to solve the problem by the means I had adopted." The criterion of larval nuclear size had in the meantime been shown to be valid. "I could not doubt that the small-nucleated larvae of my 1889 experiment had really developed from anucleate egg fragments" (56:419).

The collapse of his argument finally came through a critical analysis of the methods by which the merogons had been prepared. Delage in 1899 had already called attention to the possibility that the egg nucleus during the shaking procedure might be fragmented and thus rendered invisible although not inactive. In fact, Boveri, in 1914, during his last season in Naples, found that the egg nucleus, after shaking, may burst and thereby become undetectable in the living egg. "This result," he wrote shortly before his death, "was rather a knockout blow." He was, however, still of the opinion that the small-nucleated dwarf plutei with paternal skeleton in the 1889 experiment were truly hybrid merogonic embryos. But he no longer had a conclusive argument available to confirm this. "This result," he wrote in his last publication, which appeared posthumously, "must now be eliminated from consideration in our discussion. On no other experiment have I spent so much time as on the culture of these hybrids. And although the final scientific results, obtained after so many errors, do not appear commensurate with the energy expended, I feel that they nevertheless bring light into a dark and confused area" (56:446).

Historically the Boveri merogony experiment will always have its significance as a first attempt to define the role of the nucleus and the cytoplasm, and as a brilliantly designed experiment for the solution of a great biological problem. In its outcome, too, it ought not to be judged as pessimistically as Boveri himself did. Precisely by the weight of negative evidence, it suggested a role of the cytoplasm. In all close investigations from 1895 to 1914, Boveri and his collaborators had observed that the hybrid merogons develop *normally at first*, becoming arrested and dying only as gastrulae (fig. 8d_2). Here also, as was shown in 1902 in the case of the doubly fertilized sea urchin eggs, two basically different periods of development can be recognized. There is a first phase, up to the gastrula stage, in which the chromosomes exert only a general influence if any at all; and a second, at the time of gastrulation, in which the species specific hereditary factors in the chromosomes must come into play, requiring at the same time the collaboration of an harmonically adjusted cytoplasm. Such harmonious cooperation is provided when nucleus and cytoplasm belong to the same species, but not in these interspecific hybridizations. This postulation of two phases is the first form of the theory of phase-specific action of the genes, and at the same time it emphasizes the role of the cytoplasm. "If one designates as heredity," says Boveri, "the totality of internal conditions which achieve the unfolding of the characteristics of the new individual, this gives the cytoplasm a much more specialized significance than one often has been inclined to assume; and more than ever one realizes the absurdity of the idea that it would be possible to bring a sperm to develop by means of an artificial culture medium" (56:435). The latter hope was, as Boveri often mentioned with irony, a dream of Jaques Loeb's.

Boveri's merogony experiment has been fruitful in other directions. The sea urchin egg was of course at once rejected because of the unsureness of the shaking method. However, Amphibian eggs can be deprived of the egg nucleus and hybridized. In this material the developmental problem can be posed more broadly. It has been shown that an heterospecific nuclear-cytoplasmic combination can work differently in different organs (Baltzer, 1920, 1933; Fankhauser, 1945, 1952; Hadorn and associates, 1930, 1937).

In other directions, the original merogony concept has been extended by Briggs and King (1952, 1957) and others. In contrast to Boveri's original use of natural nuclear transplantation by means of insemination, these authors have shown that one can, with a very fine pipette, inject the nucleus of a later developmental stage into an enucleated frog egg, and allow it to develop. This new method has yielded important conclusions on the relation between nucleus and cytoplasm during embryonic differentiation.

Later, in 1936, Hörstadius invented a more reliable and at the same time more delicate method of removing the nucleus from the sea urchin egg. He cut the portion of the egg containing the nucleus away from the rest of the cytoplasm with a fine glass needle. The wound heals rapidly. In 1954, 65 years after Boveri's first experiment, L. von Ubisch used this method for producing merogons in the classical combinations of Boveri. In most of his cases the embryos did not develop beyond gastrulation; the cytoplasm could not collaborate with the strange nucleus. However, in two experiments, von Ubisch raised pluteus larvae with small nuclei and paternal skeleton. Here the nucleus had primacy in determining the skeletal form, as in Boveri's cases. Von Ubisch confirmed what Boveri had written to Spemann on May 8, 1915, after he had convinced himself of the inadequacy of the shaking method: "I do not wish to deny absolutely the possibility [of development of merogon plutei in this hybrid combination]. Often something works once with sea urchin eggs, then no more for 20 years." In older pluteus stages, von Ubisch observed maternal characters appearing in juxtaposition to paternal ones. Whether the egg in this case transmits inheritance by way of plasmagenes in the strict sense is today still an open question.

The Chromosome Theory of Inheritance,
Experiments with Doubly Fertilized
Sea Urchin Eggs (Dispermy Experiments)

If one makes the easy generalization that all great things are simple, this may apply to the idea that chromosomes carry different hereditary factors. But to prove decisively the correctness of this idea was not simple. For this purpose an artful and almost inquisitorial system of experiments was required. The experimenter had to produce egg cells with altered chromosomal arrays and had to be able to follow their development and observe to what abnormalities or peculiarities these alterations led. That appears simple. However, though the chromosome pattern is easy to observe in a fixed and stained cell, this is not true in the living state. How can it be made possible to detect the presence of an altered chromosome set and then to follow the development of the cell in question? Boveri's experiment with doubly fertilized sea urchin eggs was the first cytological procedure fulfilling these requirements.

His work up to this point had led him to three conclusions: (1) Chromosomes retain their individuality from one cell division to another. (2) The developing egg obtains corresponding chromosome sets from egg and sperm nuclei. (3) Each of these parental sets, separately, is sufficient for normal development of the germ. Given that these three facts identify the chromosomes as carriers of hereditary substance, two opposite possibilities present themselves. Each chromosome may contain the total hereditary substance — this was the view advocated by Weismann — or each chromosome may be the carrier of different portions of the hereditary material. In the latter case, each chromosome would be of different genetic value, an idea that Wilhelm Roux had interjected into the discussion as early as 1883. Boveri decided this question in favor of differential value by the analysis that we shall now discuss.

The experiments were carried out in the winter of 1901-1902 and in the spring of 1905. The final, extremely comprehensive report (43) appeared in 1907. It was preceded by two excellent summaries, a first one in 1902 (29) and a second in 1903, enlarged in 1904 (32, 34). As was often the case with Boveri, an already

---

FIGURE 9. Development of dispermic sea urchin eggs. Double fertilization is relatively frequent in artificial fertilization when a large quantity of sperm is added. *a*. Fertilization of egg by two sperm with 18 chromosomes each. Schematic. N, egg nucleus with 18 chromosomes. *b*. Doubly fertilized egg with four-poled division figure. Drawn from life. The dispermic egg contains 54 mother chromosomes (not visible in the living state), from which derive 108 daughter chromosomes. *c* and *d*. Fixed tetrasters, chromosomes stained. Examples of unequal chromosome assortment: *c*, equatorial plate stage, not all chromosomes shown; *d*, anaphase. One sphere receives only 14 of the 108 elements, the others 26, 32, and 36 respectively. Of the 6 elements recognizable by their hooked shape, two spheres receive 2, the others only 1 each. Spheres schematic. *e*. The tetraster has developed to a four-celled stage ("simultaneous four"). Note the different size of the nuclei, as is regularly found in tetrafoils. In this case, the nuclear size has been calculated from 9*d*. Centrosome schematic. *f*. Doubly fertilized egg with three-poled figure (triaster). From life. Chromosomes not visible. *g*. Fixed triaster, stage of separated daughter chromosomes. Here also the 108 daughter chromosomes are, in the main, unevenly divided. Each pole receives on the average a larger number of chromosomes than in the case of the tetraster, in this case, 31, 35, and 42. *h*. The triaster has divided into a "simultaneous three." Centrosomes schematic. Figures 9*c*, *d*, and *g* from Baltzer (1909 and 1911); others schematized.

SCIENTIFIC WORK

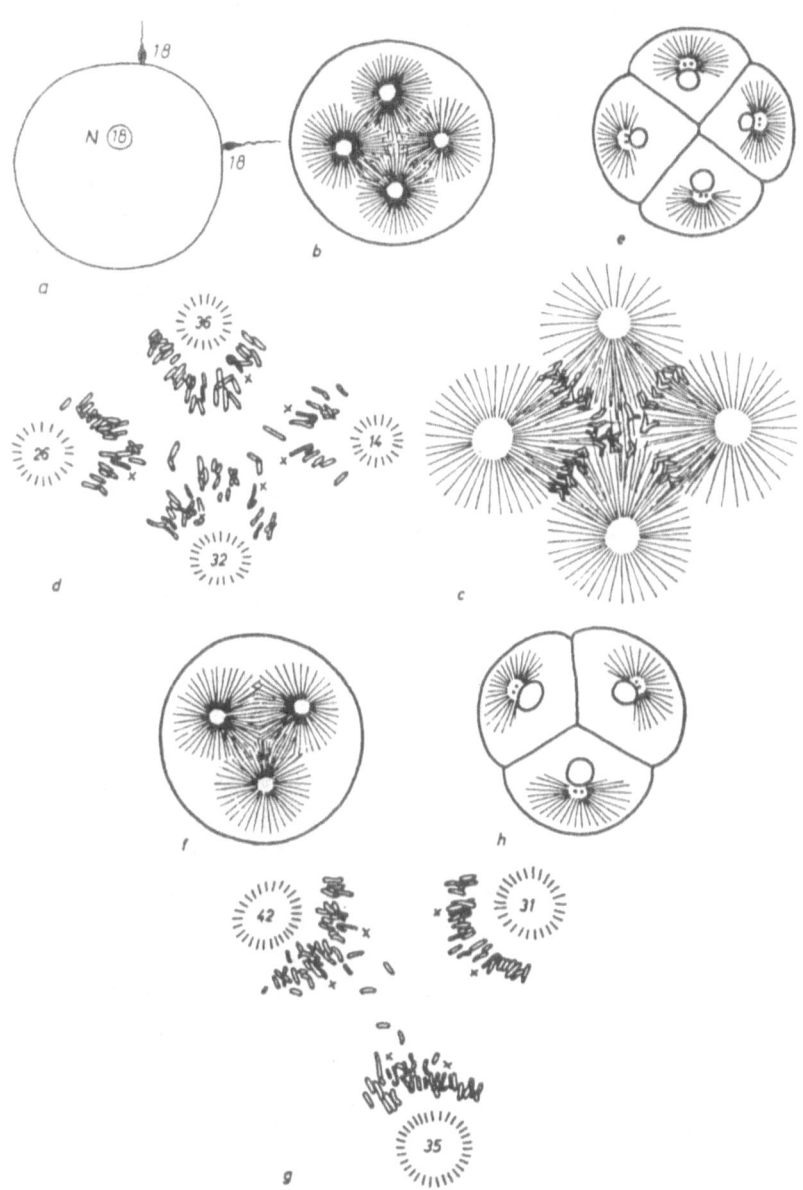

known developmental anomaly gave him the key to these experiments. In cultures of artificially fertilized sea urchin eggs, one often finds "simultaneous fours." In these cases, the egg divides immediately into four cells, without passing through the normal two-celled stage (fig. 9c). The division itself proceeds from a four-poled astral figure, a "tetraster" (fig. 9b). Such tetrafoil cleavages appear when the egg is fertilized simultaneously by two sperm (fig. 9a). As Boveri found in 1888 (8), in normal fertilization the egg engulfs a centrosome or division organ along with the sperm head. The centrosome divides and forms the two centers of the first cell division spindle (see fig. 1b and c). In the doubly fertilized eggs, two sperm enter the egg. Consequently, four centrosomes are formed, and hence a tetraster. Boveri felt that this was strong evidence for the correctness of his centrosome theory of fertilization, and that conversely the theory could explain all anomalies of the dispermic eggs. It was for him "an example of how the disclosure of a single new fact [the discovery of the sperm centrosome] suddenly can illuminate a quite distant area, hitherto dark" (43:28).

Concerning the fate of these tetrafoil cleavages, it was known according to the work of Driesch (1893 b) that they at first develop normally, then unexpectedly die during gastrulation. Driesch did not discuss the cause of this. Boveri however realized that in tetrasters the chromosomes must almost always be distributed unequally to the four cells. The decisive point is that the chromosomes are bilateral, and can be related to only *two* centrospheres. In the bipolar spindle this guarantees equal distribution to the two poles. However in dispermic eggs, *four* centers compete for each chromosome. Chromosome distribution must thus occur at random and for the most part unequally. An irregular set, once established, would be repeated in subsequent divisions. Fixed tetrasters, with the chromosomes stained, later reinforced this view (Baltzer, 1909, 1911). In figure 9c and d examples of such division figures are reproduced.

The implications for the developmental potency of the embryo

Plate 1. Theodor Boveri at the age of 27. Munich period, 1889.

Plate 2. August Pauly, 1901.

Plate 3. The *Seehaus* at Höfen. This photograph was taken prior to 1903, when the building was enlarged.

PLATE 4. Theodor Boveri, 1897.

PLATE 5. Frau Marcella Boveri, née O'Grady, 1897.

PLATE 6. Theodor Boveri in his laboratory in the institute, Würzburg, around 1907.

and its four separate blastomeres are clear: If each chromosome contains all hereditary factors necessary for the development of the different organs, then an unequal chromosome distribution should cause no defect in development. If, however, the chromosomes as carriers of heredity are qualitatively different, then with unequal chromosome distribution there will be germ regions lacking certain hereditary factors. This would express itself in pathological development, either in premature death of the whole embryo or in developmental defects in one or more quadrants. In other words, the study of the tetrafoil cleavages should show whether the whole hereditary substance is contained in each chromosome or whether it is distributed to different chromosomes.

We have previously indicated that the basis for this reasoning can be found as early as 1888 in Boveri's second *Cell Study* (8). At that time, he found occasional cases of *Ascaris* eggs with tetrasters. An especially good example is shown in figure 6, and it can immediately be seen that the chromosomes will be unequally distributed to the four poles. Boveri closes the commentary on this case with the statement that the nuclei of the resulting daughter cells must receive different qualities, "in case we are to ascribe different qualities to the individual chromatic elements" (8:869). This idea remained with him. He returned to it (16) in another article on fertilization in 1892. But it was the special advantages of the dispermic sea urchin eggs that allowed him to proceed with experimentation.

From the first tetraster observations a second possibility, the production of triasters, quickly emerged. Morgan had already found in 1895 that instead of tetrafoils one often obtained trefoils if the eggs were shaken shortly after insemination. Obviously the shaking interfered with the division of one of the sperm centrosomes, and thus three instead of four spheres were produced. In a tripolar figure (fig. 9*f*, *g*, and *h*), the possibilities of a more equal distribution of chromosomes naturally are greater than in a tetraster. If Boveri's basic assumption were correct, he should get better development from such trefoils from the fours. As we shall see, this assumption was fulfilled beyond the most optimistic expectation.

Before we compare these two experimental groups, we must turn our thoughts in another direction. The cardinal point of the discussion up to now has been the unequal distribution of the chromosomes. But since the egg cell possesses, in addition to the chromosomes, an extensive cytoplasmic body, another question must be posed. Does differential division of the cytoplasm possibly play a part in the pathological development of the tetrafoils and trefoils? To test this question, Boveri separated from one another the blastomeres of normal four-celled eggs. This can be done very safely by placing the eggs in calcium-free sea water according to the method of Herbst (1900). He then raised these isolated "quarter embyos" to test their developmental potency. When he started with normal four-celled stages, well developed plutei, that is, artificial quadruplets, resulted. The first four blastomeres in normal development thus are equivalent in cytoplasm and in chromosome array. They also possess, as will be detailed later (fig. 12, p. 108), equivalent portions of the various cytoplasmic layers. This last is also true for the tetrafoils (and trefoils). Here also, the cytoplasm is separated by the first division into morphologically equivalent cleavage cells. Nevertheless, in isolation, most of the tetrafoil blastomeres die as blastulae; others, less numerous, as gastrulae; and almost none even attempt to form a pluteus. For the isolated blastomeres of the trefoils the same is true, although in this case normal development is more frequent. It was clear, then, from the isolation experiments, that *cytoplasmic* differences were not responsible for the altered fate of the isolated cells of the tetrafoils and trefoils.

The successive phases of this experiment, carried out by Boveri and his wife in the winter of 1901–1902 in Naples, are graphically depicted in letters to Spemann. The Boveris obtained decisive results with enviable rapidity. After two months the outcome was clear. The idea of using dispermic eggs to determine the qualitative unlikeness of the chromosomes proved exceedingly fruitful.

> I have raised the four blastomeres of simultaneous-tetrafoil eggs in isolation. Most important, as a rule a different thing happens to each cell. One goes to pieces at the blastula stage, one forms mesenchyme and then goes *kaputt*, another begins gastrulation or even completes it. Once I even got a pluteus — admittedly somewhat rudimentary. Taking everything into consideration, I believe that here we are finally closing in on the nucleus. That the development does not depend on quantity of chromatin but on quality is quite certain [December 1, 1901].

Then two and a half months later, on February 17, 1902: "After I had followed the isolated blastomeres, I returned to the development of the intact dispermic eggs, finding that these do not always die as stereoblastulae, as Driesch stated, but that one gets — rather rarely — gastrulae and even abnormal plutei.

"Fortunately there is another type of dispermy where the relationships are much more favorably displayed. If one shakes the eggs shortly after insemination, many of them form a three-poled figure with simultaneous division into three cells, as Morgan had observed without being able to explain the significance." For these trefoils, as Boveri expected, the chances of correct chromatin distribution are more favorable.

> We have raised at least 500 such trefoils in isolation; among them were some twenty absolutely normal larvae, and, from these, all imaginable gradations down to the usual pathological stereoblastulae. These larvae demonstrate clearly that the *quantity* of chromatin is entirely irrelevant. I have a few larvae in which one third contains tiny little nuclei, the other two thirds much larger ones. The boundaries between the two areas can be demonstrated with extraordinary precision. Nevertheless the morphology of the larva is not affected by these boundaries. On the other hand, highly pathological monsters are often found showing nuclei of the same size in all areas.

"Moreover I beg you," he adds in this letter to Spemann, "not to say anything about the dispermy experiments for the time being. The fact is, if only one thinks of it, the experiment is easy to do. It is in any case simpler," he continues with bitter humor, "than to steal a pocketbook from an inner coat pocket, as recently happened to me in the jostling of a crowded tramcar — unfortunately the pocketbook had 230 chromosomes in it. This affair afforded me the privilege of looking through the album of pickpockets — a handsome gallery — at the central police station. But I was not able to find mine in the array."

Boveri's statement that it is a simple thing "if only one thinks of it, to do the experiment" may occasion a short commentary. Boveri's creative concept of the dispermy experiment is an extremely striking example not only of acute thinking, but also of imagination. Its power lies in the intuitive integration of highly disparate data: the death of the dispermic germs, the centrosome theory of fertilization, the distribution by chance of the chromosomes in the multipolar division figures, and the idea of the chromosomes as carriers of diverse hereditary factors. This power of intuition is not necessarily unexpected in so extraordinarily artistic a man as Boveri.

Let us turn now to a more precise calculation of the chances for normal development in dispermic eggs. In other words, how frequently will all four or all three cells receive a complete chromosome set? The eggs of the sea urchin species used contain, in normal fertilization, 36 chromosomes, 18 from the egg nucleus and 18 from the sperm. The two arrays are alike. Boveri's arbitrary assumption was that all 18 chromosomes carry different hereditary factors. Accordingly, the chromosomes may be distinguished as numbers, 1–18. The dispermic eggs contain two sperm nuclei and one egg nucleus, thus three sets of chromosomes 1–18. It was required to calculate with what frequency each cell in the original tetrafoil or trefoil would contain at least one representative of each chromosome type 1–18.

Following the advice of his friend Wien, the physicist in Würzburg, he devised a simple chance-calculating apparatus to determine these frequencies. The three chromosome series 1–18 were represented by 54 numbered balls, three balls marked with each of the numbers. The balls were mixed in a cup and poured at random onto a circular plate with a frame superposed, dividing it into three or four compartments as the case required. For the tetraster calculation a rectangular cross was used, for the triaster counts a triradiate frame. The number of balls in the individual sectors was counted. A total of 200 throws was made for each of the two types. The results were that in the tetraster distribution, 64 percent of the cases showed all four quadrants as "defective," that is, in no quadrant were all 18 chromosome types present. In 34 percent one quadrant, and in 2 percent two quadrants, contained the complete assortment. Cases with four normal quadrants for the tetrafoils did not occur in the 200 throws used.

In the triaster tests, however, the result was different. Here, in 11 percent all three thirds were complete, in 42 percent, two, and in 36 percent only one. Entirely defective cases with three

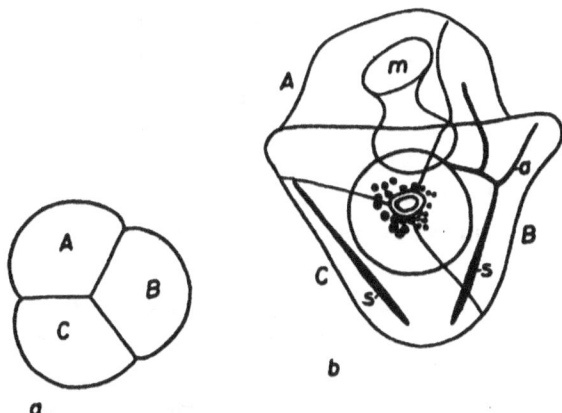

FIGURE 10. Development of pluteus with skeletal defect from a "simultaneous three." *a.* Diagram of the trefoil with cells A, B, and C. *b.* Pluteus in same orientation as 10*a*. Each sector has uniform nuclei, shown only in the anal region. Note especially small size of nuclei in sector B and absence of skeleton in sector A (m, mouth; s, apical rod; a, anal rod). From Boveri (43), Figure 31.

incomplete chromosome assortments occurred in only 11 percent. In biological terms these figures mean, assuming that in the sea urchin egg all 18 chromosomes of the haploid set carry different genetic factors and that all are required for a normal pluteus, that normal larvae may be expected practically not at all from tetrasters; but from triasters about 11 percent of the eggs should develop normally. This expectation was strikingly confirmed in the experiment. Of 1500 tetrafoils individually cultured, a single one developed into a healthy pluteus (0.07 percent); from 719 trefoils, 58 perfect plutei or 8 percent resulted (43:157 f.). If one includes defective plutei, the number rises to 79, or 11 percent.

In addition to the cases where normal plutei developed, the partly inhibited embryos were of interest. The defects and anomalies they showed were almost always limited to circumscribed sectors of the body which corresponded to the three or four original cells. We shall consider only the trefoils in detail. According to the statistical prediction, one of the trefoil cells would contain a complete set in 36 percent of cases, and two cells in 42 percent. Thus embryos normal in one or two thirds of the body are to be expected with corresponding frequency. Morphological examination confirmed this expectation, with special impressiveness in the case of skeletal defects. An example is shown in figure 10*a* and *b*. Here the skeleton in one third of the body is lacking. In many cases, as in the example figured, it can be ascertained from the size of the nuclei that the limits of this defect coincide with the limits of one of the original three blastomeres (fig. 10*b*). Translated into terms of chromosomes, this means that in such cases the particular chromosomes containing the factors requisite for normal formation of the skeleton must have been missing from that particular body region. Which of the 18 chromosomes are involved, the experiment does not say. Here the sea urchin experiment had reached its limit, a limit that the work on *Drosophila* was the first to surmount.

A final fact that we anticipated in connection with the hybrid merogons (p. 83) should be mentioned. Most of the dispermic

SCIENTIFIC WORK

eggs develop abnormally. The pathological phase, however, begins only in the blastula, or at the beginning of gastrulation. Cleavage is normal. On these grounds, Boveri distinguished two developmental phases. Not until the onset of gastrulation do chromosomes exert their specific individual influences, for which specifically adjusted cytoplasm is requisite. In the dispermic eggs, development becomes pathological because of the absence of certain chromosomes; in the case of the hybrid merogons, because the paternal chromosomes belong to a foreign species.

Let us conclude. By the assumption of a differential genetic significance of the chromosomes, a large number of facts observed by Boveri in his dispermy experiment can be brilliantly explained. This assumption forms a keystone in the construction of the chromosome theory of inheritance, the first foundation of which had been laid by Rabl and Boveri 15 years previously with the theory and the evidence for the individuality of the chromosomes. One understands the judgement of Wilson (57:75), quoted here with some omissions:

> One who, like the writer, had puzzled in vain over the riddle presented by the double-fertilized eggs of sea urchins could not read Boveri's complete and beautiful solution without a thrill. This result, wholly new, . . . is fundamental to our entire view of the cytological basis of heredity. As is often the case with discoveries of the first rank it gives at first sight little suggestion of its far-reaching importance or the difficulties that had to be surmounted in its attainment. It brings forward the long-sought crucial evidence of the direct influence of the nucleus [chromosomes] in determination and development; all attempts to shake the force of that evidence have proved unavailing.

And one also understands the reproach that Goldschmidt makes to contemporary biology (1959:110), that it is "scarcely conceivable that this classical experiment is completely passed over in many genetics textbooks of the present day."

Boveri's theory was rapidly supported by conclusive facts. It was already known that single elements of a chromosome set may have different form and different size, and that these differences are repeated regularly through subsequent divisions. Nevertheless, as Boveri, speaking as a cell physiologist, correctly put it, "The more our insight grows, the more we realize that in these questions the *morphological* is only the foundation for what we ultimately want to know: namely, what *physiological properties* are attributable to these chromatin elements which undergo so dramatic a history" (32:30; 34:91). Some physiological facts were already at hand. Various investigators, chiefly the Americans — proceded however by Henking (1891) — had found in insects a single, morphologically identifiable chromosome, obviously concerned with determination of sex. In these cases the male forms two sorts of sperm cells, different in their chromosome content. If the egg is fertilized by one sort, a male develops; fertilization with the other type yields a female.

To these findings on insects, similar ones on various nematode species were later added by Boveri, his students, and other workers (47). Parallel situations were later found in humans, butterflies, *Drosophila*, and many other forms. With the discovery of such "sex chromosomes" and the information that they carry numerous genetic factors, a simple explanation was at hand for sex-linked inheritance, as for example, color blindness in man.

On the other hand, there are species in various animal groups in which a bisexual generation, with separate males and females, regularly alternates with an hermaphrodite generation. The chromosome cycle of these forms, which include the threadworm *Rhabditis nigrovenosa*, interested Boveri particularly. "The problem," he says, "that is set by this developmental cycle, is clear. If there are two different sorts of spermatozoa, distinguishable by their chromosome number, one determining the female, the other the male sex, why then do fertilized eggs [of the generation with separate sexes] develop into individuals of only one type [the hermaphrodite generation]? And how can such an individual form both sperm and eggs? And how, among these sperm, can two different types reappear, distinguishable by their chromosome content?" (52:84). The problem formulated here by Boveri was independently and simultaneously solved by Schleip (1911). In *Rhabditis*, this alternation of sexual generations is achieved by specialized chromosome divisions in sperm maturation, deviating from the normal type.

The same line of thought is found in one of Boveri's last works, concerned with the special reproductive pattern in bees. As is well known, the workers and the queen develop from fertilized eggs, the drones from unfertilized ones. In addition to these three types there are, in exceptional cases, hermaphrodite bees (*Zwitterbienen*) in which both male and female characters are combined. For an explanation, Boveri assumed that the eggs in this case, as in the females, were fertilized, but that the sperm nucleus, retarded, finally united with one of the daughters of the egg nucleus. In 1888 he had described such an anomaly in sea urchins as "partial fertilization" (7). Only 26 years later did he have the opportunity to test his hypothesis in bees. The apiarist Eugster in Constance had supplied a famous collection of hermaphrodite bees to the zoological collection in Munich. Boveri investigated the mosaic of male and female characters in Eugster's bees. "The view," he concluded, "that the hermaphrodite bees originate by so-called partial fertilization has a probability closely approximating certainty" (55:298).

The Cytological Basis of Mendelian Phenomena, The Boveri-Sutton Theory

In the last pages we have considerably anticipated the state of research at the beginning of the century, and must retrace our steps. Generally considered, the problem of heredity had been attacked from two angles, by the cytologists beginning in the '70's, and then in a completely different fashion by Mendelian research. We need not further characterize the cytological approach since Boveri's works form milestones of this road. The study of Mendelian heredity, genetics in the strict sense, developed independently of the cytological findings. This resulted from the publication of experiments by the botanists Correns, de Vries, and Tschermak in 1900, and Correns' rediscovery (1900) of Mendel's work (reprinted, 1901). The method of genetics lies in a systematic analysis of varietal hybrids, which can without difficulty be bred further for many generations. The basic and well known result was the recognition that hereditary constitution lies in numerous independent units, the genes.

A further important result was that the genes in diploid organisms, such as higher plants and almost all multicellular animals, are present in two assortments of which one is transmitted from the father, the other from the mother. These double gene sets are reduced to the single state during the formation of germ cells. The further breeding of the second and third generations of hybrids shows that the genes do not blend, but remain pure, since in the second hybrid generation the characters of the pure original races reappear, and furthermore reappear in definite numerical proportions.

Let us return to the cytological foundations. Several investigators, led by Boveri and Sutton, called attention to the astonishing correspondence between the cellular and the Mendelian results. From this parallel arose the theory that the chromosomes are carriers of different gene groups, a concept discussed by many authors in those years.[12]

[12] The attribution of this important theory may deserve a short comment. Boveri made his first report on his dispermy experiments in 1902, with only a short reference to the results of the botanists on the behavior of plant hybrids (that is, Mendelism). He discussed the theoretical bearing in detail in a summarizing report in 1903, a lecture which appeared enlarged and illustrated in 1904. Finally, in 1907 he published the whole dispermy material in detail with extensive discussion.

In the years 1902 and 1903 two articles by Sutton appeared. The two authors published independently. Boveri's approach was physiological, concerned with the different values of the chromosomes in development. Sutton's approach was morphological, based on the constant differences in size and form of the chromosomes of the grasshopper *Brachystola*, the behavior of the germ cells, and in particular of the sex chromosome during maturation.

We may state the parallels briefly. The autonomy of the Mendelian genes, detected by hybridization experiments, corresponds to the autonomy of the chromosomes, as recognized by the individuality theory and observed in the germ line during embryonic development. The double sets of genes in diploid organisms correspond to the double chromosome arrays in the fertilized egg cell. In addition, the reduction of the diploid gene sets to the single haploid complement in gamete formation has a parallel in the behavior of the chromosomes in this phase. Finally, Mendelian segregation and its numerical relations are explained cytologically by the processes during the reduction divisions and the stages preceding reduction.

This last, most striking correspondence may be reproduced in Boveri's own words and illustrated by the schema of figure 11.

> The corresponding qualities D and R of two varieties enter the hybrid independently side by side. As Mendel has clearly recognized, they are again separated cleanly from one another in the hybrid germ cells. As is seen from the numerical ratios, this has the simple result that half of the egg cells contain D and the other half R, and the same is true for the sperm cells. Only under this hypothesis, according to the laws of probability, will the three possible combinations DD, DR and RR occur in the proportion 1 DD:2 DR:1

In contrast to Wilson's book, which formulates the theory as founded by "Sutton and Boveri," we have given Boveri the first place, taking account of a comment by Boveri himself in 1907: "It is written in almost all publications on this subject," he says, "that Sutton and Boveri have spoken for qualitative difference of the chromosomes. However, one need only read the first sentence of Sutton's paper (1902) to find that he knew and used my results. It is equally incorrect to say that I followed Sutton in the idea that the different value of the chromosomes is to be correlated with the Mendelian data. I do not doubt that Sutton has independently become aware of this relationship." In fact, Sutton begins his first paper with a reference to Boveri: "The appearance of Boveri's recent remarkable paper on the analysis of the nucleus by means of observation on double-fertilized eggs has prompted me to make a preliminary communication of certain results obtained in a general study of the germ cells of the grasshopper *Brachystola magna*." Thus it seems most appropriate to give Boveri precedence.

Boveri's 1902 paper has appeared in English translation in *Foundations of Experimental Embryology*, edited by Willier and Oppenheimer (Englewood Cliffs, N.J.: Prentice-Hall, 1964).

RR, that is, exactly the ratios in the Mendelian law. Let us imagine one character located on a chromosome D of one parent, the other on the homologous chromosome R of the other parent; then all offspring of the first (hybrid) generation will have the combination DR in their nuclei. In reduction, in oogenesis and spermatogenesis,

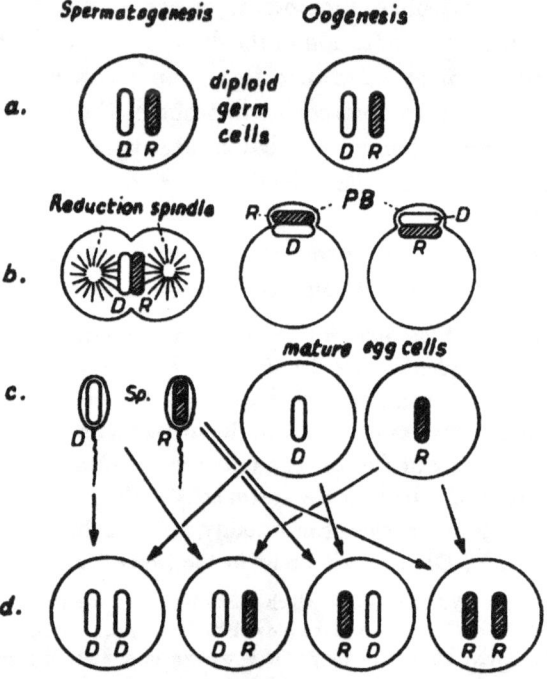

FIGURE 11. Diagram of chromosome reduction and Mendelian segregation. *a*. Diploid primordial germ cells with two chromosomes. The chromosome derived from the mother carries gene D; that from the father (shaded), gene R. *b* and *c*. Reduction of chromosome set to half by maturation divisions (in the interest of simplicity only one division is shown). The maternal and paternal chromosomes separate and are distributed without any blending to the future sperm cells, or to the egg and the polar body (PB), the latter considered as an abortive egg. Corresponding segregation of the two genes. *d*. Diploid recombination of the chromosomes with genes in fertilization. Note Mendelian ratio — 1 DD : 2 DR : 1 RR. Original.

these homologues, united on the reduction spindle [fig. 11*b*], will again be passed singly to different sperm and egg cells. Exactly half the sperm receive D, the other half R, and the same holds for the eggs. And now the same holds true that was described above for the recombination of characters in the Mendelian experiment. Roughly, the new combinations of D and R must occur in the ratio 1 DD:2 DR:1 RR, that is, in the proportion of the Mendelian rule. We thus see two research fields, developed independently of one another, coming to conclusions that correspond so closely that one might have been deduced from the other; and when we consider what we have inferred from other facts concerning the significance of the chromosomes in heredity, the liklihood becomes extraordinarily great that the characters followed in the Mendelian experiments actually are bound to definite chromosomes. [32:30; 34:115ff.]

Boveri rightly placed great reliance on these correspondences, and, on their basis, formulated a series of postulates and predictions, as early as 1903 and 1904, that may be cited here in the light of subsequent research developments as examples of his theoretical power.

From 1910 on, the American workers, following Morgan's discovery of *Drosophila*, found in this fruit fly an object with unequalled possibilities, both for genetic analysis and for chromosome work (Morgan, *et al.*, 1925; Dunn, 1951; Friedrich-Freska, 1961). Its chromosome number is small; the haploid set contains only four elements. These are, compared with *Ascaris* chromosomes, inconveniently small in most of the organs of the fly's body; but in the salivary glands these same elements enlarge a hundredfold or more, developing into giant chromosomes.

A first important step occurred when Bridges in 1916 was able to show, in abnormal maturation divisions in *Drosophila*, that the egg might receive an altered chromosome set. Definite alterations in visible, inherited characters followed these chromosomal alterations. Thus the hope expressed by Boveri in the dispermy paper that "methods would be found by means of which abnormal chromosome combinations could be obtained in controllable conditions" was fulfilled (43:243).

Another important prediction of Boveri's concerns linked inheritance, a third, the exchange of chromosomal segments. When "two characters, in later generations, always occur together, or are absent together," this would "with greatest probability permit the conclusion that the factors for both of these characters are localized on the same chromosome" (34:118). On the other hand, it "would indicate an exchange of parts between the homologous chromosomes" if characters, the factors for which are localized on the same chromosome, are yet capable of separating. Both predictions have been fulfilled. Furthermore it was found, again in *Drosophila*, from analysis of degree of linkage, that genes in the chromosomes are arranged in linear series. Maps have been prepared with precise values for these linear distances. The order is constant for each one of the four chromosomes, each chromosome having its own pattern. On the other hand, beginning in 1933, a corresponding linear fine structure was found in the giant salivary gland chromosomes. The genetic and cytological results, taken together, form a brilliant enlargement of Boveri's thesis of the differential value of the chromosomes.

Thanks to the size of the salivary gland chromosomes, genetic problems can also be approached from the chemical point of view, a research direction that in the last decade has been reinforced by genetic investigations on viruses and bacteria. With some slight exaggeration it can be said that the center of interest now no longer lies in the chromosomes, but in one of their major components, the nucleic acids.

As early as 1904 in the article on the constitution of the chromatic substance, Boveri expressed his opinion on the role of chemical investigation in cytology. He did not believe that the cellular components designated by biologists as chromatin, plastin, protoplasm, and so on, should be turned over completely to the chemist.

F. Miescher, the distinguished founder of cell chemistry, prophesies in one of his last letters in the year 1895 that mighty battles would take place in the twentieth century between morphologists and biochemists over the question of nuclear constitution and the associated problems of heredity. His whole life work attests clearly enough to his conviction that the victory would go to his own discipline. The morphologist also will have enough self-abnegation in his desire for understanding to hope for the final victory of his opponent. Even he can think of no happier situation than that morphological analysis should arrive at the point where its ultimate elements are definable chemical individuals.

At that time, this desired goal, namely to identify the ultimate morphological elements as chemical individuals, seemed to him "more distant than ever," and he asked if "such a goal, in the sense that the ultimate *essential* elements of living material are chemical bodies, really exists" (34:123). It is of no little significance that even today the morphological view persists side by side with the purely chemical. Admittedly it has been removed to the macromolecular scale; the nucleic acids in themselves are the concern of the chemist. But the endless complications of their molecular structure and the possibility of their replication according to a defined pattern belong among the problems of the chemically oriented geneticist. The problem of *developmental* genetics, in which not only the chromosomes but also the structure of the cytoplasm must be implicated, is admittedly not solved hereby.

The work on the development of the doubly fertilized sea urchin eggs had led Boveri not only to the general biological conclusions already described, but also, as early as 1902, to the problem of the origin of malignant tumors. He conjectured that malignant tumors develop as a consequence of abnormal chromosome combinations. It is just such irregular configurations that lead to degeneration in the dispermic sea urchin experiment. At the same time, these investigations had shown that abnormal chromosome combinations are irreparable, whereas damage to cytoplasm can as a rule be regulated. Also, in tumor tissues, multipolar mitoses, which lead to irregular chromosome distribution, are frequent. All this seemed to make the cancer problem one of nuclear constitution rather than of cytoplasm.

The hypothesis published in 1902 by Boveri found little approbation among the medical profession. Nevertheless, twelve years later, Boveri again took it up and defended it further in a special article (54).[18] "I have," he says in the introduction to this paper, "for a long time made efforts to approach my concept experimentally, up to now without success, but nevertheless unshaken in my conviction." This 1914 paper is one of the very few cases in which Boveri, the supreme advocate of demonstrable facts in the experimental field, entered so minutely into an undemonstrable hypothesis. However, he said, one should "again think through the idea of the relationship between abnormal mitoses and malignant tumors." As a zoologist, he also justified his writing on a medical problem in a fashion so characteristic of Boveri the scientist that we reproduce part of it here.

> I have no experience worth mentioning in any of the many special areas of cancer research; instead, my knowledge is almost exclusively from books. This being the case, it is inevitable that I should exaggerate the significance of many facts and value others too little. This article undoubtedly will have even more serious deficiencies, as are often found when an author invades a field foreign to him. One might ask how anyone who says this of himself can believe that he has anything worthy of notice to offer to investigators who have devoted years and decades of work and thought to the riddle of cancer. There is, however, one consideration: *the tumor problem is a cell problem*; and it is at least not impossible that a biologist who has sought the real basis of living phenomena in cells, may have had his attention directed to properties essential to the tumorous state but not to be derived from the study of tumors themselves. With this consideration I should like you to entertain what follows [54:2].

[18] This paper was translated into English by Marcella Boveri under the title *The Origin of Malignant Tumors, by Theodor Boveri* (Baltimore: The Williams and Wilkins Company, 1929).

SCIENTIFIC WORK

Boveri's hypothesis proposes as a cause for the beginning of a malignant tumor "a particular, incorrectly combined chromosome array. This is the cause of the tendency to proliferate, which is passed on to all descendents of the original cell, insofar as they multiply by regular mitotic division" (54:22). The means by which the abnormal chromosome complex is derived is, as in the sea urchin embryos, multipolar mitosis, whether spontaneous or released by chronic damaging stimuli.

Boveri could not verify the correctness of his hypothesis, and during the fifty years following its publication it has been neither confirmed nor refuted. It is true that in malignant tissues multipolar mitoses are often found, but a proof that such mitoses are primary to the formation of a tumor has not been obtained.

With these considerations directed to medicine, we may close the first section of Boveri's work, devoted to the chromosome theory; the reader will not object to the detail in which the dispermy experiments in particular have been reported, in view of the significance that they still retain.

II. Investigations of the Constitution of the Egg and the Collaboration of Cytoplasm and Nucleus in Embryonic Development

As we have explained in the preceding section the chromosomes are carriers of hereditary factors. In fertilization they are supplied in almost identical sets by the parents to the zygote from which the offspring develops. But the zygote in addition obtains from the mother an extensive, highly organized egg cytoplasm which plays a significant role in embryonic development. The works of Boveri to be considered in the present section are devoted to this cytoplasm, its structure, and its cooperation with the nucleus.

Wilson (57:80) wrote in an appreciation after Boveri's death that the latter had "sometimes been placed with those who ascribe a 'monopoly of heredity' to the nucleus. He it was, nevertheless, who first gave an experimental demonstration of the determinative activity of the protoplasm in ontogeny." What in fact bears witness to Boveri's genuine scientific greatness is that he was not deluded by the results of his chromosome studies, but recognized the *interplay* of nucleus and cytoplasm during development as a problem of equal magnitude. Wilson continues: "As early as 1892 he concluded that the form of cleavage is determined wholly by the protoplasm of the egg. . . . In later years he gave increasing attention to the role of the protoplasm in development, returning to this problem again and again in successive works. Some of these are among his best."

In this area also Boveri's two objects of investigation, the eggs of the sea urchin and of *Ascaris*, rendered him crucial service. For the sea urchin egg, the important works appeared in 1901 and are, quite apart from the observations themselves, of interest because of the controversy with Driesch, the champion of modern vitalism. The first observations on *Ascaris* were published as early as 1887, and the major works in 1899 and 1910. The work on the sea urchin will be considered first.

On the Structure, Development, and Potencies of the Sea Urchin Egg

The cleavage of the sea urchin egg is a famous example of the way in which, at the commencement of ontogeny, the fertilized egg develops by regular divisions (cleavages) from the one-celled condition into a harmoniously organized multicellular embryo. These transformations, even including the appearance of the first organ primordia, can be followed with great clarity in the living egg under the microscope.

Morphologically the mature egg has a typically polar structure; an animal and a vegetative pole can be distinguished (fig. 12*a*). Fertilization is followed by two meridianal cell divisions. Thus, first two and then four daughter cells are found, each containing corresponding segments of the animal and vegetative cytoplasm (fig. 12*b* and *c*). This equivalence of the first four cleavage cells is, as we previously saw in the development of dispermic eggs (p. 90), of great significance. The third cleavage,

SCIENTIFIC WORK

however, cuts equatorially and results in four animal and four vegetative cells (fig. 12*d*). The divisions then proceed differently in these two parts. The animal cells form a circlet of eight cells of uniform size; the four yolky vegetative cells cut off four very small yolk-free cells, the micromeres (fig. 12*e*). In this way, the first organ primordia may be recognized. In normal development the circlet of eight cells yields the material for the body wall of the larva; the four intermediate cells form the digestive tube; the micromeres the supporting skeleton (see fig. 10*i*). With surprising regularity, about ten hours after insemination, the egg has developed into a hollow ball, the blastula (fig. 12*f*), and again ten hours later into a gastrula with a simple gut and early skeletal primordia (fig. 12*h*). A day later the culture dish is full of thousands of transparent swimming pluteus larvae about a third of a millimeter in length (fig. 12*i*).

So regular and constant a series of events might encourage the view that sea urchin development is determined from the beginning, in the sense of the preformation theory. This easily controllable and experimentally available material was evidently suited to give an essential contribution to the centuries old embryological problem. The question of preformation had again been posed a few years earlier by Wilhelm Roux (1888) with reference to the frog's egg. He killed one of the blastomeres of the two-celled stage with a hot needle. The undamaged sister cell developed into a *half embryo*. This spoke, at first, for preformation. In 1891, Driesch repeated this experiment on the egg of the sea urchin, *Psammechinus microtuberculatus*. He shook eggs in the two-celled stage. In many cases the two sister cells were separated and could be raised independently. "The isolated half-cells," wrote Driesch (1951:74), "did in fact cleave as if they were still connected with their sisters, and formed half-cleavage stages resembling half of a hollow ball. However, this then closed to a small whole ball, and I obtained on occasion, quite contrary to my expectations, a dwarf pluteus." The same result occurred, though with greater difficulty, in the development of isolated

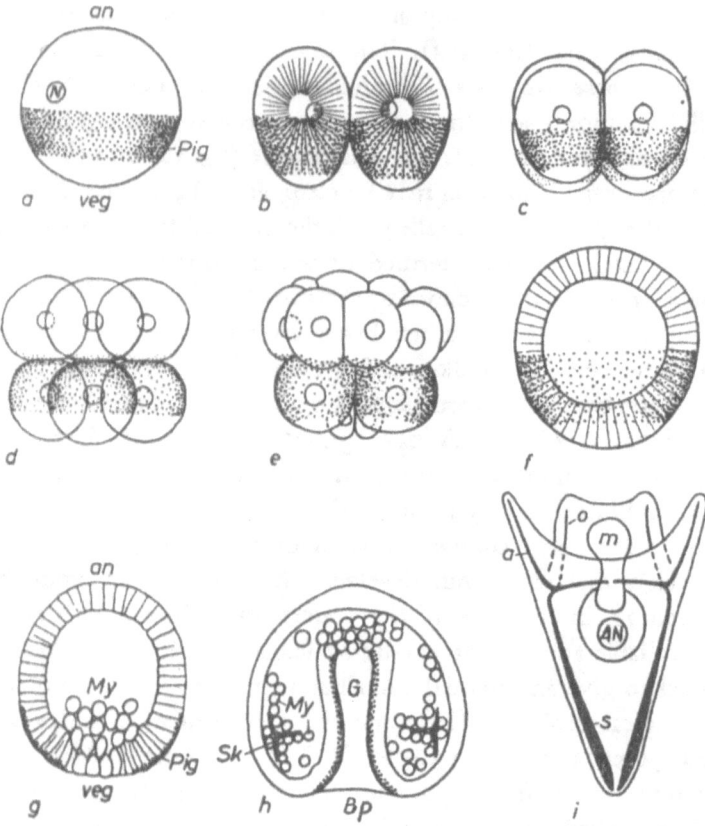

FIGURE 12. Development of the sea urchin egg (*Paracentrotus*) to the pluteus stage (*a–h* oriented with animal pole upward; *i* shows anal view). *a*. Fertilized egg. N, nucleus with maternal and paternal chromatin; an, animal pole; veg, vegetative pole; Pig, the orange pigment ring, visible until larval stages. Total, from life. *b*. Two-celled stage with daughter nuclei and asters. Total, from life. *c*. Four-celled stage. Nuclei of lower cells stippled. Each of the cells has an equivalent part of the pigment ring. Total, from life. *d*. Eight-celled stage (two cells out of view). The pigment ring is almost entirely segregated into the four vegetative cells. Total, from life. *e*. Sixteen-celled stage (eight animal cells, four vegetative pigmented cells, and four unpigmented micromeres). Animal cells will form the body wall, pigmented cells

¼ blastomeres. "One can," Driesch reported, "remove at will material from cleaving eggs, provided the remainder is not less than one quarter of the whole, without losing the potency to develop" (1893a:25). In his view, then, to take a simple example, a cellular region that normally would have formed larval body wall, should be able experimentally to become gut wall, and vice versa. This implies totipotency of the cells.

This experiment led Driesch to his vitalistic concept of living processes. If every portion of the egg or germ can "almost without limitation" form the whole organism, this cannot be explained mechanistically any more than it could be thinkable that in a machine, physical or chemical, composed of different parts, a *part* of the machine could produce the work of the whole. "I was taking a solitary walk in the Zurich woods [in the year 1895], when the thought suddenly came to me that the results of my experiments on embryonic development and regeneration obviously had left a very weighty problem unanswered in regard to physico-chemical or 'mechanistic' causality. One can cut up a thousand-celled embryo *at will* and from the fragments obtain the whole organization as the result of development" (1951:108). Such systems, in which the whole can develop from a part, Driesch called "harmonic equipotential systems," equipotent since each

---

will form gut, and micromeres the skeletogenous primary mesenchyme. Total, from life. *f.* Young blastula, with animal and vegetative halves and blastula cavity. The pigment band lies in the vegetative half. Schematized, from life. *g.* Longitudinal section of blastula at beginning of migration of skeletogenous primary mesenchyme (my) into the blastocoel. Pigment (Pig) limited to outer borders of vegetative cells. Schematized. *h.* Gastrula with blastopore (Bp). Pigment in invaginated gut (G). First triradiate skeletal spicules (Sk). Total, from life. *i.* Pluteus larva. Tripartite gut, including foregut with mouth (m); midgut; and hindgut with anus (AN). The skeleton consists of four rods: a, anal rod; o, oral rod; s, apical rod; and one crossrod. Figures 12*a–h* from Boveri (27); 12*i* original.

part can produce the whole, harmonic because the part forms anew what is required to restore the harmonic unity. The final analysis of such systems leads, according to Driesch, "not to elementary physico-chemical laws, but to elementary *laws of living matter*, to *vitalistic elementary laws*" (1898:713). In other words — and herein lies the importance of Driesch's challenge — he claims for living processes, even when they can be partially explained in physico-chemical terms, an autonomous system of laws; the harmonic equipotential system is for him the evidence of this.

It was clear that experiments of such importance should be pursued further. As often happens, improvements of method and the discovery of a more suitable object of experimentation played a decisive role. Herbst, a friend of Driesch, discovered in 1900 that the cells of the sea urchin fall apart from one another if placed in calcium-free sea water. A technique much less damaging than shaking was thus provided for Driesch's experiment, and he repeated his observations the same year with ⅛ blastomeres. But this time the result was quite different. The developmental potency of the ⅛ blastomeres was very diverse. Many developed only to blastulae, others to gastrulae, and only in uncertain cases did plutei result. Driesch did not succeed in relating these various resultant forms in any definite way to the different regions of the germ.

Here we come to Boveri's investigations of the year 1900. The eggs of the sea urchin species used by Driesch did not show polar structure with animal and vegetative regions clearly differentiated. In the spring of 1900, Boveri was experimenting in Villefranche. "In the course of other investigations," he writes (26:145), "as I was observing the eggs of *Paracentrotus lividus* more closely, I realized that the yellowish-red pigment lying beneath the surface of the egg is arranged *in a ring*."[14] He understood at once the importance of this fact, insignificant in itself. "A study of the development showed that the *egg axis* determined by the

---

[14] The pigment ring of the *Paracentrotus* egg had been discovered in 1883 by Selenka, but his observations had been forgotten.

pigment ring coincided with the axis of cleavage and with that of the gastrula. Since the possibility presented here of relating the polarity of the larva back to *a visible polarity of the egg* is of great importance for a whole series of developmental questions, I determined to inquire into the relations as far as possible." The result of these investigations, made jointly with his wife, were published in two papers in 1901. One (27) contains the morphological description of the ring and the axial relations up to the pluteus stage in the early development of *Paracentrotus*. Extraordinarily accurate and beautiful figures are included, which have remained to this day the standard morphological document for sea urchin development, and which have formed the basis for countless further experiments. The pictures in figure 12 are taken from this publication.

The second paper (26) reports the isolation experiments that Boveri now conducted to test Driesch's results. With the help of the pigment ring he could observe in *Paracentrotus*, with all precision, that ½ and ¼ blastomeres contain equivalent amounts — half or a quarter — of each sort of plasma, vegetative or animal, whereas the animal ⅛ cells contain almost none of the pigment ring and the vegetative ⅛ cells almost all of it. With these observations, Boveri linked the hypothesis of a material animal-vegetative gradient. According to his assumption, a lesser or greater concentration of this material determines the developmental capacity of the cytoplasmic region in question. The decisive point is that, in the case of such stratification, the two or four first blastomeres will receive equivalent portions of the determining materials, just as they can be seen to obtain equivalents of the yellowish-red pigment. In the formation of the eight-celled stage, however, the distribution of material is quite different. The four animal cells receive layers of material that allow development only to the blastula stage, but the four vegetative cells receive portions that permit development to the pluteus. Within the vegetative zone there are also differences. The area nearest the vegetative pole possesses the greatest potentiality to bring development completely to the pluteus stage. It is the "priority region" where differentiation begins. And when differentiation has begun, "from this center all other regions are determined in their role by a regulatory action" (26:167).

At the same time Boveri proceeded with fragmentation experiments. He found that animal fragments of the uncleaved fertilized egg were as limited in developmental capacity as were the animal $\frac{1}{8}$ blastomeres, by comparison with the $\frac{1}{2}$ and $\frac{1}{4}$ blastomeres. Animal egg fragments, containing no pigment whatever, develop, even if they are very large, only to the blastula stage. By contrast, fragments containing a large proportion of pigment, thus with much vegetative plasma, can reach the pluteus stage. Consequently Boveri, in contrast to Driesch, could not regard either the cleaving germ or the mature egg as an harmonic equipotential system; it is not surprising that he remained somewhat skeptical in regard to his opponent. "I gradually come to suppose," he wrote to Spemann in 1902 from Naples, "that Driesch has looked somewhat superciliously through his microscope." This skepticism did not affect his evaluation of the concept of the harmonic equipotential system. "I still feel it to be one of the most urgent tasks to get to the heart of the harmonic equipotential system with all the methods at our command." However he added the Mephistophelean query "whether harmonic equipotential did not mean carelessly examined."

About 25 years later the development of the sea urchin was reinvestigated by Hörstadius (1928) with a much more perfect technique. He succeeded, with very fine glass needles, in cutting the eggs without damage and with accurate orientation, and in raising the parts in isolation. He also succeeded in systematically combining cleavage blastomeres of different origin. Hörstadius too concluded that the sea urchin egg as a whole is not an harmonic equipotential system.

Boveri's thesis of stratification of hypothetical substances exerted a great influence on the course of further research, especially as refined physiological-chemical methods became available.

This idea was the forerunner of the gradient hypothesis of the Swedish school of developmental physiologists, and was moreover the precursor of the concept of the organization center elaborated 23 years later by Spemann. For theoretical purposes, Boveri's views substituted an intelligible mechanistic concept for Driesch's postulated vitalistic factors in embryonic development.

If the controversy between Driesch and Boveri is interesting because of the fundamental biological questions touched on, it is no less fascinating when considered in relation to the personalities of the two investigators.

Driesch, born in 1867 and originally a student of Haeckel, possessed an extraordinary gift for biological experimentation, but at the same time a theoretical bent so pronounced that considerations of theory took precedence over facts. His theoretical gifts led him to philosophy, though he said himself, "When I decided to became a natural scientist, I certainly had no thought whatsoever of philosophy. Indeed I did not rightly know what it was." It is not surprising that in experimentation he lit upon the sea urchin egg. This material had by that time become famous because of the ease with which it could be manipulated. "And then," he writes, "I had 'luck'—that means a favorable stimulus came from outside—precisely that the sea urchin egg was able to put up with my interventions without dying." Isolated cleavage cells developed into complete larvae, which was a fundamental result that he extended by numerous further experiments, including regeneration in other forms. From 1891 on, in uninterrupted and ingenious inventiveness, he sought fuller support for the vitalistic views he had elaborated in the meantime. He had begun, he narrates, with "the experiment stage"; this was followed "in the second phase by the clear conviction of the *teleological* nature of everything organic." In a third phase, Driesch created the concept of the harmonic equipotential system, and on this basis proclaimed "the autonomy of the organic, so-called vitalism" (1951:286 f.). Driesch's experimental period lasted from 1891 to 1909. Then he turned entirely to philosophy. In 1909 his major theoretical biological work, *The Philosophy of the Organic*, appeared.

The strength as well as the weakness of Driesch lies perhaps in the preponderance of theoretical thought over observation. When Boveri, with composed objectivity, corrected the factual content of Driesch's experiments and broadened those experiments themselves, this meant nothing crucial for Driesch when weighed against the great vitalistic concept. It is characteristic of him that in his *Philosophy of the Organic* he reiterated the results of his experiments and scarcely recognized the objections of his critic. Here, to borrow one of his phrases, the decisive factor was the "surrender to an idea" (1951:304).

Boveri, five years older than Driesch, was as a scientific personality less self-assured and much more cautious in relation to the object of his investigations. Theoretical speculation for him remained subordinate to the facts, and the value of a theory was for him decided by the material with which it could be established. No less a born experimenter than Driesch, he was by contrast more at home with morphological methods of investigation. Thus, as a more accurate observer and critical thinker, he could not remain blind to the errors and uncertainties of the demonstration of his opponent, while at the same time respecting his great contributions. Boveri's commitment toward organic form is clearly seen in the precision of his figures illustrating sea urchin development, figures to which the shabby depictions used by Driesch in describing his experiments stand in flagrant contrast.

The Problem of Embryonic Differentiation, Analysis of Diminution in the Development of Ascaris

In 1888 Boveri, as we showed in an earlier section, had found decisive evidence for the individuality of the chromosomes in *Ascaris megalocephala*. A year earlier, the same material had already informed him that the chromosomes in a portion of the cells of this worm actually do not maintain their individuality (5). In fact, in developmental stages the large loop-shaped chromo-

SCIENTIFIC WORK

somes persist in only a single series of cells. In all other cells, the ends of the loops are cast off and resorbed in the cytoplasm; only the middle part of the loop remains, falling apart into numerous tiny chromosome fragments. This diminution, "one of the earliest, as it is one of the most beautiful of [Boveri's] discoveries" (Wilson, 57:72), is pictured in figure 13. In this section, we consider only theoretically important aspects — the problems of germ-line and embryonic differentiation. For details the reader is referred to the explanation in figures 13 and 14.

Boveri was immediately and rightly of the opinion that the cells that did not undergo diminution would later give rise to germ-cell material, thus constituting the germ line, whereas the cells showing diminution would compose the body or "soma" of the worm: gut, musculature, integument, and other organs. It was to be expected on theoretical grounds that the germ cell series would contain intact chromosomes, since by these the total hereditary constitution would be passed on to subsequent generations.

In figure 14 the contrast between germ line and soma is presented schematically. The former, to use an expression of Boveri's, has rights of primogeniture. Its cells, with intact chromosome loops, give rise, through five cell divisions, to two primordial germ cells (fig. 14, PGC), which form the material of origin for the tremendous number of eggs and sperm to be found later on. At the same time, these cell divisions yield somatic cells as well. Figures 13*e* and *f* and 14 indicate what develops from each.

After discovering the basic facts, Boveri concerned himself for over twenty years with the problem of diminution. The major publications were in the years 1899 (23) and 1910 (50). Intervening shorter communications (1892, 1904, and 1909) show how the analysis grew step by step out of the original purely cytological observations.

With the discovery of the germ line in *Ascaris*, Boveri immediately encountered a problem that had been under discussion for decades. As early as the '60's, Weismann, Metschnikoff, and Leuckart had found, at one pole of the developing insect egg, the

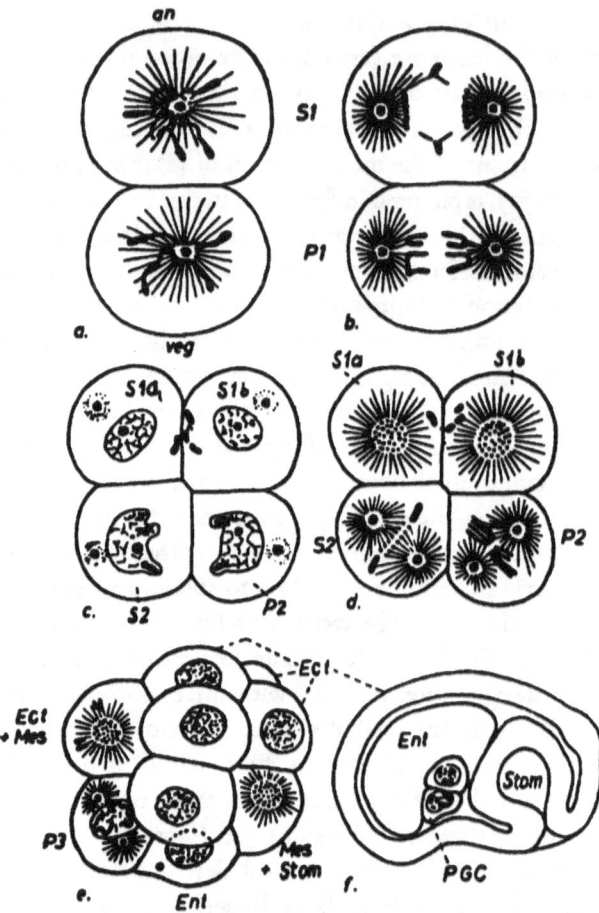

FIGURE 13. Diminution of chromosomes and development of the egg of *Ascaris megalocephala* univalens. *a* and *b*. Two-celled stage (an, animal pole; veg, vegetative pole). *a*. Equatorial plate in polar view. Diminution of chromosomes in the yolk-poor animal cell, S1. Chromosomes remain intact in the yolk-rich germ line cell, P1. *b*. Anaphases in lateral view. In S1, daughter plates formed of diminished chromosomes. The cast-off chromosome ends remain in the cytoplasm. In P1 the intact chromosome loops have separated. *c* and *d*. Four-celled stage. *c*. Interphase nuclei. Both S1 cells (S1 a and b) have rounded, dimin-

"primordial germ cells," and had concluded that these elements gave rise exclusively to sperm or egg. On these observations Weismann (1885) and others had based the theory of the germ plasm. This states that, as a general rule in ontogeny, the germ cell material descends in an unbroken line from the egg through to the formation of the gametes, thus remaining independent of the soma. This proposition has a very important consequence from the phylogenetic viewpoint, which was worked out with great acuity by Weismann in particular. If the almost quiescent germ line and the functioning somatic organs are so independent of one another, an inheritance of somatically induced characters is unthinkable.

Boveri's observations furnished a fundamental piece of evidence for this germ line theory, since by reason of the diminution phenomenon in *Ascaris*, germ-line and somatic development could be followed with unprecedented clarity, cell for cell. In particular, the great study of 1899 has remained one of the most distinguished works in this field and was dedicated by Boveri to his former teacher, the anatomist Carl von Kupffer. The 1899 paper includes exemplary illustrations, which show all of Boveri's love and painstaking care in morphological matters.

The process of diminution in *Ascaris* posed still another prob-

---

ished nuclei. Of the two vegetative cells, one (S_2) will show diminution, the other (P_2) will retain the germinal character. *d*. Early anaphase. The somatic cells S_1 a and b and S_2 have diminished equatorial plates (S_1 in polar view, S_2 in lateral view). Only P_2 retains intact chromosomes. *e*. Twelve-celled stage. The germ-line cell P_3 shows the two typical primordial chromosomes. The somatic cells will regularly form ectoderm (Ect), mesoderm (Mes), mouth area (Stom), and entoderm (Ent). Cf. Figure 14. *f*. Longitudinal optical section of embryo. Mouth area (Stom) formed. The two primordial germ cells (PGC) with intact chromosomes have been overgrown by ectoderm. Figures 13*a–d* from Boveri (34), figures 26–29; *e* and *f* from Boveri (23), figures 14 and 33*a*.

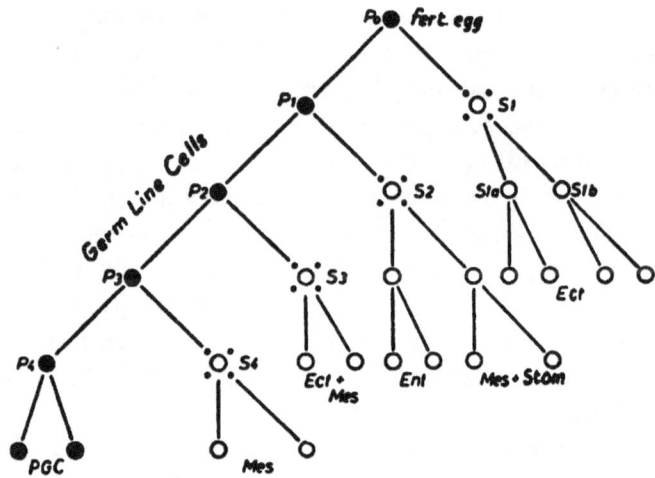

FIGURE 14. Schematic representation of the development of germ line and somatic (body) line in *Ascaris*. The fertilized egg undergoes four successive divisions in which a germ-line cell (P_1, P_2, P_3, P_4) is segregated from a primitive somatic cell (S_1, S_2, S_3, S_4). In the fifth division, P_4 divides into the two primordial germ cells (PGC). The somatic cells meanwhile divide into daughter cells that will form various body regions — ectoderm, mouth area, mesoderm, and entoderm. From Boveri (50), p. 135.

lem, lying at the point where embryology and genetics intersect. This was the problem of differential nuclear division and, in this connection, of embryonic differentiation. Every egg develops rapidly by cell divisions to a multicellular body whose cells originally look much alike. Then differentiation sets in. Some cells develop into muscle cells, others to gut cells, still others into nerve cells, and so on. They become different in cytoplasmic structure as well as in nuclear type.

If one seeks the cause of this differentiation, one faces a paradoxical situation. The multiplication of cells is bound to the mechanism of nuclear division, and this mechanism provides that all cells shall obtain the same chromosome set, that of the fertilized egg. How then, if the chromosomes are carriers of heredity, is development into different cell types possible? For cells to differentiate in various directions, must not the hereditary factors first be distributed differentially?

In fact, Weismann as early as 1885 had proposed that the nuclear substances, that is, the chromosomes, might be systematically altered during ontogeny. The simplest assumption would be that "in each nuclear division the specific plasma of the nucleus would be divided, according to its nature, into *unequal* moieties [that is, the chromosomes would be divided unequally], so that the cell bodies, the character of which is determined by the nucleus, would thus be new-stamped" (1892:223). Weismann recognized that the observations of Strassburger (1884) and van Beneden (1883) spoke for an identical, not for differential, chromosome division. Nevertheless, according to him, Strassburger had "clearly overestimated the certainty of the observations;" as against van Beneden one should not forget "that what we see there is not the molecular structure of the nucleus" (1892: 225 f.) Boveri's great chromosome work of 1888 (8) also spoke against Weismann's hypothesis. The differentiation problem remained unsolved. Here Boveri's further analysis intervened. Diminution in *Ascaris* could be chief witness for or against autonomous differential division of the chromosomes, and had already been interpreted by zur Strassen (1896, 1898, 1902) in Weismann's sense.

Boveri, by contrast, sought the cause of diminution in the cytoplasm. He had already made the suggestion, in 1899, that doubly fertilized *Ascaris* eggs might present a possibility of deciding; but not until 1904 (35) had he "found a number of decisive cases." To these cases, amplified by the examination of centrifuged eggs and also eggs irradiated with ultraviolet light, the large work of 1910 (50) is devoted. The work was dedicated to Richard Hertwig on his 60th birthday.

In the introduction to this article, one of Boveri's best, he describes how to work with the *Ascaris* material, which he kept constantly at hand in Würzburg.

Perhaps it may seem doubtful whether it is worth while to employ this material, until now so obstinately immune to experimental influence, for studies in developmental mechanics. And I must confess that, were Würzburg on the seacoast, other objects and problems than those here examined would have captivated me. But for one who finds his supreme scientific gratification primarily in investigating the processes by which a new individual, with definite qualities, arises from the parental reproductive material, and who must

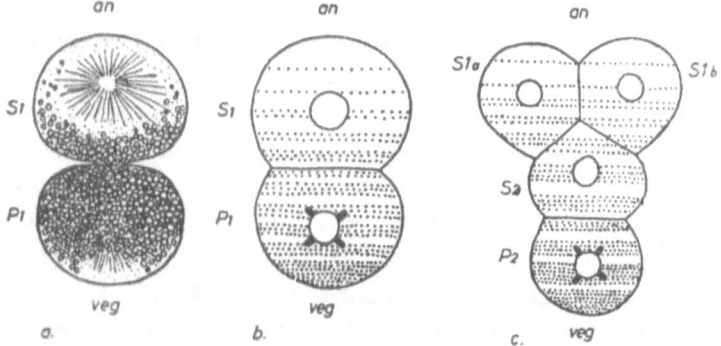

FIGURE 15. *Ascaris megalocephala*. Normal cleavage. *a*. Two-celled stage with yolk-poor animal cell, S1, and yolk-rich vegetative cell, P1 (an, animal; veg, vegetative pole). From life. *b*. Two-celled stage with schematic rendition of the hypothetical cytoplasmic gradient. The diagram assumes that the vegetative cytoplasm contains a high concentration of germ-cell determinants. Here the chromosomes remain intact, and the nuclei retain the lobes where the chromosome ends lie. In cytoplasm with lower concentrations of the hypothetical material, the chromosomes undergo diminution and the nuclei are rounded, without lobes. The schema shows the univalens race with two chromosomes. *c*. Four-celled stage. Cells S1 a, S1 b, and S2 with lower concentrations of the hypothetical substance have nuclei of somatic type. The cell with the highest concentration retains the P character. Figure 15*a* from Boveri (50), Figure A; 15*b* from Boveri (50), Figure Y*a*; 15*c* adapted from Boveri (50), figures B and O.

always expect interruptions in his study of the living object, *Ascaris* forms an unsurpassable material. The eggs can be stored for some months, dry, in the cold, without alteration. When one has time for work on them, this can be done at room temperature, where they continue to develop slowly. If one wishes to accelerate development temporarily, one brings the eggs into an incubator. If one must interrupt work, one puts them back in the cold, and, on returning, one finds them in the same condition in which they were left. And in addition to the natural experiments of giant embryos [the result of fusion of two eggs] and double fertilization, some workable experimental techniques have gradually become feasible, such as selective destruction of parts of the germ by ultraviolet light, or centrifugation of the developing egg. Other methods will doubtless be added to these. Thus the *Ascaris* egg has full right to be placed with the classical objects of embryological experimentation" [50:133].

As is seen in figure 15*a*, the *Ascaris* egg in normal cleavage first divides into two cells with unequal cytoplasmic content, one animal, with little yolk, and the other vegetative and rich in yolk. In the first mitosis the vegetative cell nucleus retains the original or germinal chromosomes, while those in the animal cell undergo diminution. The same is repeated in the second cleavage, and can be seen in the four-celled stage. Only the most vegetative cell (P_2 in fig. 13*c*) retains the germinal chromosomes.

According to Weismann and zur Strassen, diminution is a process intrinsic in the chromosomes and independent of the cytoplasm, whereas according to Boveri it is conditioned by the cytoplasm. Boveri's hypothesis was that the *Ascaris* egg cytoplasm contains a substance, differentially distributed in animal and vegetative regions, that determines the behavior of the chromosomes. The distribution of this unspecified substance is in the form of a concentration gradient, diagrammed for normal development in figure 15*b* and *c*. The question of the chemical nature of the substance was not pursued by Boveri, nor has it been opened since. On the other hand, Boveri discussed thoroughly the matter of the gradient and its distribution. But this was not the essential point for him. What was new was that cytoplasm could *in any way* determine the character of the nucleus; the advantage of the *Ascaris* material was that it permitted such an effect of the cytoplasm to be observed.

Here let us turn to the doubly fertilized eggs, which have given the strongest evidence for the correctness of Boveri's hypothesis; and let us take the variety bivalens (see fig. 2) with four chromosomes as an example. According to Weismann's hypothesis, normally, in the first mitosis, there must be derived, from the four original chromosomes, four daughter chromosomes of the non-diminished or germinal type, and all four must remain together in the vegetative cell P_1. The same must occur in the second cleavage mitosis. The cell P_2 must receive four germinal chromosomes.

The doubly fertilized, still undivided egg receives six original chromosomes, two from the maternal nucleus, and two from each sperm. When the fertilized egg then divides simultaneously into four cells, according to Weismann's hypothesis a total of *six* germinal chromosomes must always result. In addition, since Boveri had already shown in 1888 that, in the tetraster, distribution was a matter of chance, "it [must] not infrequently happen that the same cell receives both germinal and somatic chromosomes" (50:173). But neither the first nor the second expectation was fulfilled. Doubly fertilized eggs often possessed fewer or more germinal chromosomes than six. "On the other hand," wrote Boveri, "I have never observed eggs in which the same cell contains both germinal and somatic chromosomes." Accordingly, diminution cannot be preformed in the chromosomes. The dispermic figures lead solely to the conclusion "that the decision whether a chromosome should or should not undergo diminution depends on the cytoplasmic nature of the cell" (35).

A simple dispermic case is shown in figure 16. In this tetraster (a), two spheres lie in the vegetative region of the egg, and the chromosomes associated with them are of the germinal type as indicated. Both these cells will become P cells (fig. 16b). In this case there will be two germ lines, one with three, the other with one germinal chromosome.

If, however, the tetraster lies so that only one aster is in the animal region, only one animal cell as against three germ-line

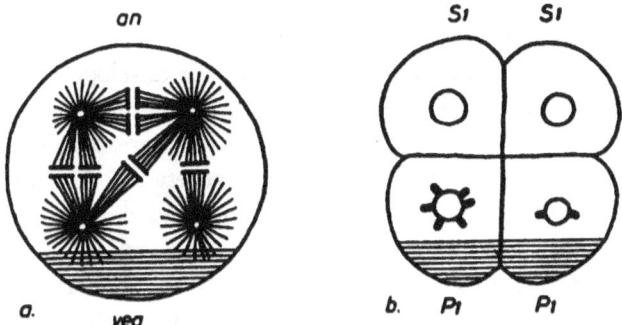

FIGURE 16. *Ascaris megalocephala* univalens. Cleavage and diminution of a tetraster egg with two germ lines. The assumed P-determining substance is indicated by shading in the vegetative region. *a.* Position of the tetraster in the uncleaved egg. *b.* The simultaneous-four arising from 16a. The upper S1 cells contain diminished, round nuclei; the two lower P1 cells, non-diminished, lobed nuclei. The P1 nucleus of the left cell contains three chromosomes; the one on the right, one. From Boveri (50), figures Y*a* and *b*; modified.

cells will be expected. This case, as well as the reverse, with three soma cells and only one of the germ line, was found by Boveri. The dispermic eggs thus decide against the autonomous differential chromosome divisions postulated by Weismann and zur Strassen. Boveri wrote in 1910:

> If my results contradict those of zur Strassen in very essential points, nothing is farther from my purpose than to misjudge the high value of his work. Rather, I truly admire, in spite of a considerable contrast in our research principles, the perspicacity, audacity, and consistency with which zur Strassen has erected his complicated theoretical construction on the basis of a few insignificant facts. One thing to be deplored is that the factual foundation on which the edi-

fice was raised was not only very scanty but also in many places quite unsteady. To establish *facts* seems to me the most important task in this field, and I do not doubt that the hypotheses of zur Strassen actually will lead to important questions shaping further experimental investigations of this material [50:209].

Boveri sought further criteria to elucidate the role of the cytoplasm in diminution. He found these in the development of centrifuged or irradiated eggs. We shall limit discussion to the centrifugation experiments. When the egg was centrifuged, during the first cleavage, in the exact animal-vegetative direction, two germ lines appeared. Diminution commenced only in the four-celled stage. The material or materials on which diminution depends are thus capable of being displaced by centrifugation. This again speaks against autonomy of the nucleus in diminution, since it is the cytoplasm primarily that is affected by centrifugation. The assumption of a material gradient gives a good explanation of this result.

In regard to the problem of the factors determining the further differentiation of the somatic cells into different types (muscle, gut, and so on) once the original decision has been made by diminution, Boveri does not relinquish the old view of Weismann and Roux that, after diminution, it would be "the now *differentiated chromatin* that reacts by imprinting some cells as somatic, others as reproductive cells. It seems to me that the case of *Ascaris* offers the simplest paradigm for the way in which reciprocal action of cytoplasm and nucleus in ontogeny is to be conceived. Extremely slight heterogeneities in the egg cytoplasm may act as release mechanisms for the nucleus, followed by feedback (*Rückwirkung*) from the nucleus to the cytoplasm, finally to produce such prodigious differences among the resulting cells" (50:191).

Let us look back. The series of studies on diminution in *Ascaris* is one of the astonishing examples of the way in which Boveri, starting from a primary important observation, would describe larger and larger circles, discovering experimental possibilities and proposing new theoretical viewpoints. Moreover, the series is an example of the patience with which he continually pursued his subject, lost nothing from sight, and did not fear being forestalled by other workers. In short, Boveri could wait for the investigation to mature and to become detached from him, as it were, by its own growth.

The first observations on diminution in *Ascaris*, published as early as 1887, were of purely cytological nature. These observations were immediately at hand since Boveri was concerned, in those years of the second *Cell Study*, with *Ascaris* chromosomes, and diminution is easily observed as one searches through sections of *Ascaris* egg-tubes for cleavage mitoses. Then a series of new questions transformed the original cytological problem into an investigation of the whole embryogenesis of *Ascaris* (1899). As a result, the question of germ line and soma came into the foreground. After this, the problem was again transformed to one of relation of nucleus and cytoplasm in ontogeny (1904-1910). Boveri's 1910 paper reflects clearly the difficulties of the question, which still remains a central one in cell biology. In summing up Boveri's contribution, one can do no better today than to quote the words of Wilson (57:88):

> No more than his predecessors did Boveri arrive at a complete understanding of the functional relations of nucleus and protoplasm in the process of determination. What he accomplished was to enlarge our view of the problem, to render it more accessible to direct experiment, to build up our knowledge by a series of discoveries of which all were important and some were fundamental; and it may be doubted whether in these respects anyone of our time accomplished more than he to advance our intimate knowledge of development and the manner of its determination.

The differentiation problem has subsequently remained in the center of research. Its solution is closely bound in with the analysis of fine structure in both chromosomes and plasma. Highly valuable insights on the problem of interaction of chromatin and cytoplasm are being yielded by electron microscopy and microchemistry on the one hand, and especially suited objects of investigation such as the giant chromosomes of *Drosophila* on the other.

III. BOVERI THE COMPARATIVE ANATOMIST

Along with his chromosome and cytoplasm studies, Boveri maintained a continuing interest in comparative anatomy, which we shall see generalized in the Rectoral Address. This interest led to his discovery, in 1890, of the excretory organs of *Amphioxus*.

The little lancelet fish, *Amphioxus*, or *Branchiostoma* as it is now called, is an awl-shaped, sand-burrowing animal about six centimeters long, classified in early days as a marine worm, later as a true fish, and finally as the most primitive type among the whole group of Chordates, of which the Vertebrates are the highest representatives. *Amphioxus* as a simplified form of this group would naturally be of special interest to a comparative anatomist. Like fish, the creature has gill slits and a uniformly segmented body musculature; and, like the lowest fish and all Vertebrate embryos, it possesses a rodlike, dorsally placed organ of support, the notochord. On the other hand, a vertebral column, bony skeleton, braincase, head, vertebrate mouth, and appendages are all missing. Whether these characteristics are primitive in the phylogenetic sense or are at least in part secondary simplifications for adaptation to sedentary life is still not clear. The animal, buried in sand except for the anterior end, feeds on suspended organic material in water brought in by ciliary action.

Structure and development of this remarkable form had been studied intensively by outstanding workers, but no organs comparable to the vertebrate kidney had been found. Boveri perceived that the previously described genital chambers in *Amphioxus* must correspond to the embryonic kidney tubules of Vertebrates. "This idea," he reported, "led me to seek pronephric tubules in a definite location, and indeed to find such structures in precisely this place" (13). As Spemann emphasizes, the discovery of these organs, so difficult to observe, was not simply a lucky chance for Boveri, "but, as almost all of his discoveries, the result of his thoroughness and acuteness in thought and observation. He found it because he looked in the right place" (57:28). In figure 17 these organs are reproduced after one of Boveri's classical drawings. They were discovered simultaneously by F. E. Weiss (1890), using a vital staining technique, though the latter author did not make a closer study.

The analysis of these organs was, as Boveri himself recognized (36:600), "very essentially extended" in one point by Goodrich (1909). Boveri described conspicuous long-stemmed "thread cells" (fig. 17, TC), which the English author recognized as "solenocytes," that is, hollow tubes with beating flagella in the lumen. "I had the opportunity of observing the flagellar action of the solenocytes," reported Boveri, "in a living preparation that Professor Goodrich was so kind as to demonstrate to me in Naples." These solenocytes bear a startling resemblance in structure to the cells of the same name discovered by Goodrich in the nephridia of segmented worms (*Annelida*). Boveri was obviously disconcerted not to have recognized the nature of the thread-cells himself. The psychological factor he designated as the cause may be mentioned here. "That I did not recognize this structure was certainly the consequence of my not *expecting* it." In fact, it was completely unexpected that a form related to the Vertebrates should possess an organ characteristic of worms. The comparative significance of the *Amphioxus* nephridia in relation to the Vertebrate kidney is, in fact, still a difficult problem.

The discovery of the nephridial tubes in *Amphioxus* was also of general importance for the interpretation of the vertebrate head, a problem that had engaged comparative anatomists for a long time. According to Gegenbaur (1888), the whole lengthy gill region of *Amphioxus* was to be homologized to the vertebrate head; according to other opinions, particularly that of van Wijhe (1889), only a short anteriormost part of the gill region was comparable. The position of the nephric canals in the posterior gill

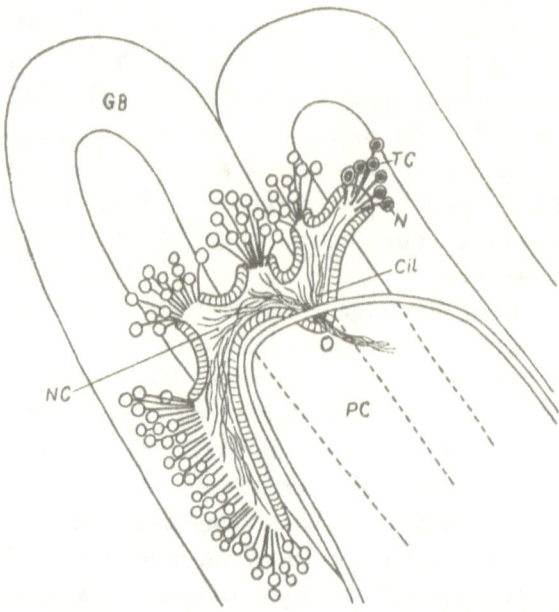

FIGURE 17. Nephridial canal (NC) of the lancelet *Amphioxus*. Beating cilia (Cil) inside the canal. Five openings into the body cavity (coelomic funnels) and one external opening (O) into the peribranchial cavity (PC). GB, neighboring gill bars. TC, thread cells (solenocytes of Goodrich, 1909), drawn in detail at the right. N, nucleus of solenocyte. From Boveri (15), Figure 1, with additions from other figures.

region spoke for van Wijhe's view; these would correspond to the pronephros in true Vertebrates, that is, to the most primitive part of the excretory system. This provided a weighty argument for the view that in the lancelet the vertebrate head is in the process of evolving.

Another concern was the particular phylogenetic significance of the photoreceptors in *Amphioxus*. These organs consist, as Hesse had discovered in 1898, of single sensory cells scattered through the whole neural tube. Each cell is provided with a pigment cap, an arrangement contrasting with the pattern of the typical Vertebrate eyecup. Boveri's article "On the Phylogenetic significance of the Visual Organs of *Amphioxus*" (37) has given us a concept of how an eyecup could have been derived from the primitive situation in *Amphioxus*.

In spite of being one of the pioneers of the now flourishing experimental research in zoology, Boveri retained a high respect for the older comparative methods and an unqualified appreciation of their significance. He experienced a kind of reverence for innate form, expressed down to the finest details of his drawings. "Thus he helped, as few others did, to develop a new era of zoological science, the causal-analytic, without belittling and losing what had been won and ascertained in the past" (Spemann, 57:28).

Other evidences show how vivid the problems of comparative anatomy and phylogeny were for Boveri. Very indicative is a detailed letter to Otto Bütschli who sent Boveri his *Lectures on Comparative Anatomy* toward the end of 1910. "In the first ten years of my teaching activity in Würzburg," Boveri wrote in acknowledgement, "I also entertained the idea of a 'Comparative Anatomy of Vertebrates' and collected material for it. But I was frustrated in this by my desire to focus, above all else, on the gradual alteration of the vertebrate body organization as a whole." Gegenbaur, the author of the classical text of comparative anatomy, as well as Bütschli, had treated the organs separately. In this way, detailed comparisons can certainly be made from group to group, but the result is neglect of the body organization as a whole, a sacrifice that Boveri found impossible. He therefore abandoned the project. Characteristically for his didactic bent, it was in his lectures that he achieved his cherished plan of emphasizing body organization as a whole. "Here," he continued in the letter to Bütschli, "it is, according to my conviction, not only justifiable, but actually preferable to the usual procedure of handling comparative anatomy by organ systems. The necessity of referring back to the preceding form when introducing a new one, is undoubtedly a useful repetition for the student, who is hearing all this for the first time. But, in the attempt to do the same thing in a book, I ran up against such difficulties that I finally gave up the whole plan."

IV. Boveri's Views on the Evolution of Living Organisms

Boveri was Rector of the University of Würzburg during the year 1906. His address at the celebration of the 324th anniversary of the founding of the university deals with a phylogenetic theme: "Organisms as Historical Beings" (42). In a sense this is the sketch of his philosophy of the organic. Here if anywhere, Boveri has followed his own principle that one must regard writing as an art. In this essay we find a plastic, dramatic diction, pertinent comparisons and captivating images, and an emotion that Boveri seldom permitted himself.

One might wonder why this master of biological experiment did not select a theme from an experimental field closer to his own investigations, and where the reasoning can be handled more rigorously than in the case of the great historical questions. He certainly was not, like August Weismann for instance, an evolutionary theorist by profession. But in this address he was one of the first to implicate findings and concepts of developmental physiology in phylogenetic considerations. Here, perhaps, lies the present significance of the essay.

The historical theme was for him the greatest biological problem, confronting science on the one hand and organic philosophy on the other. "The principle of evolution," he says, "not only dominates all thought in zoology and botany, but assigns to these disciplines their position, and determines their role in the formation of our philosophy of life [*Weltanschauung*]. A theory of life would not be valid without taking into account the historical nature of organisms." Added to this was a personal consideration. In the year 1905, the book of his friend August Pauly on Darwinism and Lamarckism was published. "After I had read it," he wrote Pauly, "I thought that the Rectoral Address would be a suitable opportunity to call attention to your work." We shall see to what degree he was able to follow the extreme psycho-Lamarckist viewpoint of his friend.

Boveri's address treats the two classical problems, phylogeny and organic adaptation. Let us consider, if only in a fragmentary fashion, the state of opinion concerning these two questions at the time when the address was given. Comparative anatomy, descriptive embryology, paleontology, and other branches of biology had by then assembled massive material in evidence of a phylogenetic evolution of organisms. The principle of evolutionary descent had scarcely any opponents remaining among zoologists. With one of the last of these, his professional colleague August Fleishmann at the neighboring University of Erlangen, Boveri sets forth a sharply worded dissent, which the reader may consult in the original.

If around the turn of the century the acceptance of the principle of phylogeny was clear, by contrast the explanation of the fact that all organisms in their structure and functions are so astonishingly well adapted to the conditions of their life, was much disputed. According to Weismann and others, the selection of favorable random hereditary variations sufficed to explain every case; somatic variations, however, disappeared because they were not inherited. According to the opinion of other investigators (Semon, Eimer, Pauly) who advocated Lamarckism in various forms, acquired somatic variations, in spite of their disputed heritability, played an important role.

Concerning his own view, Boveri questions whether any biologist growing up in the last 40 years of the nineteenth century could have failed at some stage to be captivated by the theory of random undirected variation and selection, "the all-powerful magic formula that explains all adaptations; a genuine Columbus egg, so simple that each person must wonder why he himself had not produced this ingenious thought. But then, as one began to test the Darwin-Wallace theory in concrete organic situations, its insufficiencies could no longer remain concealed" (42:17).

After Boveri's time, skepticism concerning the effectiveness of selection was removed by precise genetic and statistical analysis; also, it became clear that mutations constitute a widely distributed type of heritable variation, and, together with selection, have operated to alter species. It remained questionable, however, to what extent the major changes, that is, production of new classes and orders, could be ascribed to the same process. Even today uncertainties persist.

In his consideration of the problem of descent, Boveri follows the comparative-anatomical tradition. Addressing laymen as well as professional colleagues, he describes the basic problem in sharp outlines. The organic world shows us a complex multiplicity of the most different forms, but this plenitude can be reduced in unexpectedly simple fashion to relatively few body plans. Most unexpectedly, the anatomical body plan bears no relation to the mode of life of the organism. A whale and a mouse as functional types are completely opposite. The first has the adaptations of a large, swimming water animal, and the mouse, the form of a tiny terrestrial quadruped. They correspond, however, completely in their body plan, in their style, that of the mammal. "By recognizing this contradiction, that animals have anatomical and embryological correspondences that are unexplainable, even quite paradoxical, on the basis of the conditions of their life," the scientific mind is given the indication of the trail "following which it can hope to come nearer to the secrets of the organic world" (42:5). The trail leads to the fundamental principle of natural classification. "The basic grouping of this is, as our example shows, the degree of correspondence in all anatomical relations, without reference to similarities determined by function; even, on occasion, in complete contradiction to functional likeness." Furthermore, "we understand all characteristics of the natural system by means of the sole assumption that systematic relationship is a true blood relationship, in other words, that all forms under a systematic rubric have arisen from a common stem form by transmutations in various directions" (42:6). This implies "that organisms are transformable and have ascended from simpler states to more complex ones." Can this ascent be considered as directed toward a goal? Boveri's position is: "As surely as this purposiveness is present in individual development, so surely is it lacking in phylogeny" (42:18). In regard to the question whether the natural system leads back to a single root, Boveri remains skeptical. He does not stretch evolutionary relationships beyond the limits given by the body plans of the major groups.

To one general problem, the origin of multicellularity, Boveri devotes a broader discussion. We present this in detail since he speaks as an experimental cytologist and because the question leads to a central problem of the lecture, that of "phylogenetic agents":

> It will generally be considered self-evident that all multicellular animals at least have a common ancestry in the unicellular ones. This assumption is necessary only under the view that the unicellular animals themselves are all blood relations; this we actually cannot know. It is conceivable that organic life has originated many times and that it must always reach a state that we designate as "a cell"; and it is in no way excluded that some day a new Cuvier will demonstrate, among the Protozoa, types as varied and as incapable of being traced to a common stem as we now find in the Metazoa. Certainly in the lowest step we know, only "cells" are present. We cannot decide whether this state is merely a functional prerequisite, as for example a Metazoan must have some sort of gut, nervous system, and so on, or whether we deal here with a conformity that can be explained only by common descent [42:51].

In regard to the question of how multicellular forms originated, and through what agency, Boveri first follows Weismann. Colonial aggregations occur in various groups of one-celled organisms. The phylogenetic agent or primary alteration is relatively insignificant in this case; its implications, however, are extraordinarily great, representing the transition to multicellularity, to specialization of function, and to differentiation among cells. "It can clearly be understood from intermediate forms now living, that the first step toward multicellularity occurs when such single-celled individuals remain together after dividing; by this perception many obscurities of reproduction and development have been brilliantly illuminated." Boveri continues:

> In this connection, the mysterious purposiveness shown in the development of the egg to a complete animal, long seen as the principal characteristic of life, loses its aura of mystery. For we now know that the phenomenon here called purposiveness is not a basic property of living matter. In the life history of the amoeba there is merely a cycle, but no goal. If, however, some generations of the daughter cells of a one-celled individual remain associated for some time before they fall apart, each to reproduce a new colony, we may consider the colonial aggregate as a special stage or *goal* in the cycle. This is the more striking in those cases in which only some of the cells of the colony retain the reproductive function. In such assemblages lies the germ of the gigantic impetus that the organic world has derived from such simple beginnings.

This is the basis for the individualized life pattern of all multicellular organisms. "From a continual succession of one-celled forms, represented by the reproductive cells, there emerge from period to period, like blind offshoots, the assemblies we call individuals." Since multicellular individuals never can revert to the simple state of origin, they are able to rise to endless complications. They must, he concludes, "at the same time accept death into the bargain: in the lowest steps of organization death is unknown as an inherent property and necessary terminus of life" (42:12-13).

Boveri devotes some consideration to the relation between historical and causal explanation of biological problems. He regards historical explanation in the phylogenetic and descriptive embryological fields as immeasurably fruitful, indeed irreplaceable, objecting to the idea that historical and causal explanations are antithetical. "The historical explanation is in itself a causal one" because "a condition that is not to be understood from its immediate surroundings stands in causal continuity with a previous condition, which in itself is explicable on the basis of its surrounding conditions" (42:10). One example is the explanation of rudimentary organs by earlier stages in which the corresponding completely developed organ was able to function.

Boveri, who at one time, it will be recalled, had thought himself a student of history, made a point of exposing for his listeners from all faculties the fascinating analogies and antitheses between history of organisms and human history. Historians and archaeologists reconstruct human prehistory from buildings, implements, and inscriptions, just as paleontologists do organic history of earlier epochs from fossils. Further, when the historian reports on juxtaposed old and new copies of Roman law texts there is an astonishing parallel with the zoologist who finds evidence of the past in, for example, the organization of mammals.

However, the *means of cognizance* in the two sorts of history differ fundamentally. For human history we have at our disposal the elementary fact of man's own psychic experience, since the historian and the one who makes history belong to the same species. Our attitude toward the history of organisms is completely different. "We cannot transpose ourselves into the elements that effect the phylogenetic changes occurring in an organism, since we do not even know what those elements are" (42:16).

Before we turn from this first part of the address, Boveri's appreciation of Darwin, whom he admired equally as a scientist and as a man, should be recorded. "The merit of Darwin is often set equal to that of Copernicus, and in fact no other comparison is more suited to do justice to the intellectual accomplishment involved in the theory of evolution and to the powerful implications of this theory. As the concept of a stationary earth had to be revised to that of a ball circling the sun, so in evolutionary theory the apparently constant species is seen to be simply a transition in a changing series of forms" (42:9).

One of Boveri's most urgent suggestions to students was to read Darwin's short autobiography. In lectures, this subject might occasion his dropping his customary restraint. "On the 100th anniversary of Darwin's birth," he wrote in 1909 to Spemann, "we hung a big portrait of him, wreathed with a garland, in the auditorium, which elicited several minutes of stamping at my entrance.[15] I spoke some fifteen minutes on the significance of the day, very plainly moreover on the descent of man, which, as I heard later through Külpe [his colleague in philosophy] aroused some displeasure among the Catholics. But as I had them stand, on finishing, nobody remained seated, and the frantic stamping was resumed without objection."

The theme of the second part of the address, the problem of adaptation and its mechanism, was for Boveri of the same order as the theory of evolution itself. "What tantalizes our minds is not that organisms are subject to change, but that the changes, by human measure, are adaptive. More concretely, we are interested not in the slight alterations by which a new species can be recognized, but in those great steps crying out for explanation. Such steps have produced land animals from aquatic ones, flying from creeping forms, seeing ones from blind, intelligent behavior from instinctive drive" (42:16).

Concerning the solution of this question, Boveri remained more skeptical than many of his contemporaries. Selection of favorable mutations, in the sense of Weismann, was for him only a partial explanation. It did not seem to him very important to adhere to a definite viewpoint, whether pure neo-Darwinism or neo-Lamarckism. "Rather, we must welcome all lines of thought leading to answerable questions that can be put to nature. This will be possible at very many points, and nobody can presume to perceive them all." And elsewhere, still more skeptical, "One must indeed ask if this is not in the final analysis an insoluble problem for the human understanding. But never to finish does not mean not to progress" (42:18).

We have already emphasized that Boveri was one of the first to introduce developmental-physiological considerations into evolutionary discussion. He sought ontogenetic processes that could serve in phylogenetic development, for phylogenetic agents (*stammesgeschichtliche Mittel*), to reveal "the elementary sculptural

---

[15] German students traditionally applaud by stamping.

laws of organisms." What are the qualities that we observe in organisms? Their nature may be defined as *the conditions of their embryonic origin.*

> Even the most complicated individual begins as a simple cell, the egg. In this cell are the determinants for all the characters of the completed state. One might designate this determining complex as the elementary properties of the organism; to fathom this is our most urgent task. It can be asserted that this rudimentary substrate [the fertilized egg] is not to be thought of as a sort of conglomerate, but as a system of constructive mechanisms, from the most specialized to the most general, superposed on one another in specific fashion, so that their functions interact predictably. If a special quality is altered, the total alteration thus produced in the organism must remain in the framework of the whole, just as the shifting of a fragment in a kaleidoscope gives a different picture; different, but satisfying because of the unchanged pattern of symmetrical replication. However, if one of the most general qualities is altered, then — to retain our figure — the whole optical apparatus of the kaleidoscope is altered and the special qualities again fall into the new frame without deficiency. In every malformation something of the wonderful properties of these elementary constructive mechanisms is revealed [42:30–31].

Since Boveri considered phylogeny to be non-purposive, it is not surprising that he ascribed importance to various aspects of chance. He regarded evolutionary changes in organisms as under control of changing environments. A species, multiplying successfully, would of necessity spread out into new territories, which would offer new conditions of life. The favorable event in this case would occur when members of such a species, undergoing random genetic variation, should happen to enter a new environment to which some chance variation was adapted (42:19–20).

According to Boveri, chance also plays an important role within the organism. As an example of such internal coincidence he cites the phylogeny of the camera eye, as disclosed by comparative anatomy. Since this case furnishes a good example of a phylogenetic agent, it may be further considered here. "If a light-sensitive region of the skin, for protection, sinks in as a pit — as such protective contractions occur in hundreds of other cases — this region, originally capable only of distinguishing light from dark, will become a *camera obscura* which can provide a true picture of the outside world; hence, by coincidence (that is, *chance*), true sight is made possible." In this case, "*chance* means nothing more than the presentation of an opportunity." He then continues critically:

> The intrinsic problem, however, only commences here. It may be formulated: By means of what forces can the organism utilize such chance occurrences, presented to it by lucky coincidence? By what forces is it able, when challenged by such coincidences, to adapt to them in so astonishing a degree?
>
> Here the roads part. For some, who follow Darwin, among whom we may name August Weismann as the most consequential, chance events are the sole factors. Chance not only supplies new possibilities and requirements, but also the means of fulfillment of these needs.

But Boveri's line of thought takes another, partly anthropomorphic, direction so characteristic that we cite the complete text:

> We have at our disposal very informative considerations as to the large part played by chance in human invention. It operates indeed in the same two ways that I have adduced for the case of adaptation in organisms: first in the appearance of new requirements, and second, much more important, in the presence or appearance of new coincidences that can serve new purposes. But in human invention a third factor is associated with these two: the quality presented by chance is recognized as a means to an end and it is enlarged by previously learned modes of operation until a tool is produced that is suited to the given task.

We must, says Boveri, "according to my conviction, assume something comparable in the organism. There must lie in the organism a perception for the specific usefulness of a quality presented by chance. The organism must also be able to improve this new quality in correlation with other acquired characters already part of its general constitution" (42:26).

An interesting example of coincidence serving new purposes is given in the origin of polyembryony. In various invertebrate groups, as, for example, parasitic forms, and also in some mammalian cases, sexual reproduction is combined with asexual multiplication of the germ so that more than one adult develops from a single egg. One-egg twinning in man and the identical quadruplets normally produced by the armadillo at every birth are well-known examples of polyembryony.

Experiments on many forms have shown that normal individuals may develop not only from whole eggs but also from egg or blastula fragments or from isolated early cleavage cells. Boveri had investigated this question thoroughly in sea urchins. In the normal development of the sea urchin such potency is useless "because surely there can never have arisen a need for the sea urchin to produce its embryos from half eggs. . . . But should it ever be advantageous to form more than one embryo from an egg, as we actually find in the case of certain tapeworms (*Coenurus*), this now useless potency would then be the precondition of immediate fulfillment of that requirement; a very fine instance of the means of satisfaction preceding the need to fulfil it." Today this phenomenon is classified as preadaptation. Boveri gives the following interesting comment. The divisibility of the sea urchin egg "looks like a highly adaptive reaction, and yet is nothing but a mechanical result of the general principles of construction that are expressed in the shaping of the sea urchin larva from the egg" (42:57).

A last, more speculative example of phylogenetic agency is the origin of the venom apparatus in poisonous snakes. The rudiment of a poison fang is first a rounded projection, then becomes a groove, finally closing to a tube; the fang grows to be many times larger than the other teeth. Here also general agents can be assumed, already belonging to the "general repertory" of the organism. "One of the most common agents is the enlargement of a specially used organ, such as the fang and the poison gland. Also, the transformation of the tooth to groove and tube form is accomplished by means that we often find used in the early history of every higher organism, where a current is to be guided in a determined direction or a cavity is to be delimited from others" (42:27).

How much still remained dark, no one knew better than Boveri himself. He did not deny that the noninheritance of characters of somatic origin created difficulties for his concept. He added, however, that there are cases in which embryonic processes, originally dependent, acquire autonomous character. As an example, he cited the behavior of the "armhole" in the gill cover of the toad during metamorphosis. The opening, out of which the foreleg will protrude, was without doubt originally dependent on the extremity. Its development has, however, become independent of the foreleg, as was ascertained by Braus, since the opening develops even after the extirpation of the forelimb bud (42:59).

The psycho-Lamarckist considerations of perception and self-improvement applied to organisms must lead to the basic problem of the relation between the psychic and the physical, to the "eternal Sphinx":

> How does the psyche intensify itself in the course of phylogeny? Or shall we think of a primitive psychic potency determined in the grade of its expression only by the degree of complexity of the material system? Indeed, here the criticism may obtrude, whether chance, after being excluded for large groups of phenomena, has not finally reappeared, in the sense that there are different levels of chance events. Thus a chance event affecting a higher level thereby imposes lawfulness on all the steps beneath. . . .[16]

---

[16] Boveri amplifies this point in an interesting footnote to the published lecture: "The following simple example may serve to illustrate. Let us think of a vessel, in which balls of different sizes are continually being shaken, and in which there is an opening through which balls can fall out. We will assume that, of the balls that fall out, only the very smallest can serve an objective that we have in view. The occurrence of this favorable event is, then, in our apparatus, a matter of

Thus we terminate in a sea of questions. Presumably in a few centuries people will smile at the audacity with which we have framed theories of adaptation, considering our puny insight into the nature of living matter, and our ignorance of the actual course of adaptation in even a single instance. . . . Nevertheless, dwarfed as we may feel when we attempt entering at any point into the causal drift of the evolutionary mechanism, once we experience the impact of the whole, we sense as it were an intimation from the fathomless depths of primeval matter [42:29, 33].

The psychic point of view so markedly expressed not only by Boveri, but also by Spemann, who was in the institute at Würzburg during Boveri's rectorship, ran counter to prevailing contemporary opinion, and was by no means adopted without critical debate in either case. Both men were on close terms with Pauly. As previously mentioned, Pauly had published his psycho-Lamarckian theory in 1905 in an extensive book on which he had worked for 30 years and in which Boveri had taken a great part. The book found little response, although even today it must be recognized that it contains great ideas and a sweep of artistic presentation. Perhaps the lack of response was due to the central psychic theme. Boveri, to the annoyance of his friend, used only a portion of these psychic concepts and was well aware of the difficulties that, quite aside from the problem of the inheritance of acquired characters, lay in the relation between psyche and physis. It is to be regretted that he never discussed the question farther.

He wrote to Pauly, as he sent him the Rectoral Address:

When you have read what I say about it [your book], perhaps you will exclaim: God preserve me from my friends . . . since I unfortunately cannot hope that you will be satisfied with the concurrence that I have expressed. While reflecting on these things, I have often been struck by what you have said about the contrast in the chance. If, however, we assume that, by some accident, the opening in the vessel is so restricted that only the smallest balls can escape, the favorable event then no longer occurs by chance, now and then, but regularly, under the control of law."

manner of thinking of Cuvier and of Lamarck. I can be quite carried away by what you write, as long as I am reading; but as soon as I consider the question with my own brain, it seems otherwise to me, and above all, I see no means of attaining any certainty concerning the most important things. For months it has been a very painful thought, that there is much in my address that must displease you.

The answer of Pauly has not been preserved. From the subsequent reply of Boveri it appears, however, that Pauly roundly rejected Boveri's standpoint. "I do not after all believe," answered Boveri in an interesting and argumentative letter, "that my statement is as wrong as you say. But perhaps it will induce you to amplify certain parts of your theory in a future presentation. And now forgive me if I have offended you again in this letter. In true friendship, your Th. Boveri."

References

THEODOR BOVERI'S SCIENTIFIC PUBLICATIONS

1. "Beiträge zur Kenntnis der Nervenfasern." Inauguraldissertation zur Erlangung der Doktorwürde der Philosophischen Fakultät der Universität München, vorgelegt von Theodor Boveri aus Bamberg. *Abh. Akad. München*, Vol. 15, pp. 421–495. 2 plates. 1885.
2. "Über die Bedeutung der Richtungskörper." *Sitz.-Ber. d. Ges. f. Morph. u. Physiol. München*. Vol. 2. 1886.
3. "Über die Befruchtung der Eier von Ascaris megalocephala." *Ibid.* Vol. 3. 1887.
4. "Über den Anteil des Spermatozoon an der Teilung des Eies." *Ibid.* Vol. 3. 1887.
5. "Über Differenzierung der Zellkerne während der Furchung des Eies von Ascaris megalocephala." *Anat. Anz.* Vol. 2, pp. 688–693. 1887.
6. "Zellenstudien I: Die Bildung der Richtungskörper bei Ascaris megalocephala und Ascaris lumbricoides." *Jena. Zeitschr. Naturw.* Vol. 21, pp. 423–515, Plates XXV–XXVIII. 1887.
7. "Über partielle Befruchtung." *Sitz.-Ber. d. Ges. f. Morph. u. Physiol. München*. Vol. 4. 1888.
8. "Zellenstudien II: Die Befruchtung und Teilung des Eies von Ascaris megalocephala." *Jena. Zeitschr. Naturw.* Vol. 22, pp. 685–882. Plates XIX–XXIII. 1888.

9. "Die Vorgänge der Zellteilung und Befruchtung in ihrer Beziehung zur Vererbungsfrage." *Verh. d. Münchner anthropol. Ges.* 1888.
10. "Ein geschlechtlich erzeugter Organismus ohne mütterliche Eigenschaften." *Sitz.-Ber. d. Ges. f. Morph. u. Physiol. München.* Vol. 5. 1889.
11. "Über Entwicklung und Verwandtschaftsbeziehungen der Aktinien." *Zeitschr. f. wiss. Zool.* Vol. 49, pp. 461–502. Plates XXI–XXIII. 1890.
12. "Zellenstudien III: Über das Verhalten der chromatischen Kernsubstanz bei der Bildung der Richtungskörper und bei der Befruchtung." *Jena. Zeitschr. Naturw.* Vol. 24, pp. 314–401. Plates XI–XIII. 1890.
13. "Über die Niere des Amphioxus." *Sitz.-Ber. d. Ges. f. Morph. u. Physiol. München.* Vol. 6. 1890.
14. "Über die Bildungsstätte der Geschlechtsdrüsen und die Entstehung der Genitalkammern beim Amphioxus." *Anat. Anz.* Vol. 7, pp. 170–181. 1892.
15. "Die Nierenkanälchen des Amphioxus." *Zool. Jb.* Vol. 5, pp. 429–510. Plates XXXI–XXXIV. 1892.
16. "Befruchtung." *Erg. d. Anat. u. Entw.-Gesch.* Vol. 1, pp. 386–485. 15 figs. 1892.
17. "Über die Entstehung des Gegensatzes zwischen den Geschlechtszellen und den somatischen Zellen bei Ascaris megalocephala nebst Bemerkungen zur Entwicklungsgeschichte der Nematoden." *Sitz.-Ber. d. Ges. f. Morph. u. Physiol. München.* Vol. 8. 1892.
18. "Das Genus Gyractis, eine radial-symmetrische Actinienform." *Zool. Jb. Abt. f. Syst.* Vol. 7, pp. 241–253. 1893.
19. "Beziehungen zwischen Zellfunktion und Kernstruktur." *Sitz.-Ber. phys.-med. Ges. Würzburg.* Pp. 94–95. 1894.
20. "Über das Verhalten der Centrosomen bei der Befruchtung des Seeigeleies nebst allgemeinen Bemerkungen über Centrosomen und Verwandtes." *Verh. d. phys.-med. Ges. Würzburg,* N.F. Vol. 29, pp. 1–75. 1 text fig. 1895.
21. "Über die Befruchtungs- und Entwicklungsfähigkeit kernloser Seeigeleier und über die Möglichkeit ihrer Bastardierung." *Arch f. Entw.-Mech.* Vol. 2, pp. 394–443. Plates XXIV, XXV. 1895.

REFERENCES

22. "Zur Physiologie der Kern- und Zellteilung. *Sitz.-Ber. d. phys.-med." Ges. Würzburg for 1896.* 1897.
23. "Die Entwicklung von Ascaris megalocephala mit besonderer Rücksicht auf die Kernverhältnisse." *Festschr. f. C. v. Kupffer.* Jena. G. Fischer. Pp. 383–430. Plates XL-XLV. 1899.
24. "Zellenstudien IV: Über die Natur der Centrosomen." *Jena. Zeitschr. Naturw.* Vol. 35, pp. 1–220. Plates I–VIII. 3 text figs. 1901.
25. "Merogonie (Y. Delage) und Ephebogenesis (B. Rawitz), neue Namen für eine alte Sache." *Anat. Anz.* Vol. 19, pp. 156–172. 1901.
26. "Über die Polarität des Seeigeleies." *Verh. d. phys.-med. Ges. Würzburg*, N.F. Vol. 34, pp. 145–176. 4 text figs. 1901.
27. "Die Polarität von Oocyte, Ei und Larve des Strongylocentrotus lividus." *Zool. Jb. Abt. f. Anat. u. Ont.* Vol. 14, pp. 630–653. Plates XLVIII–L. 1901.
28. "Das Problem der Befruchtung." *Verh. d. Naturf. u. Ärzte 1901.* Separate and expanded. 48 pp., 19 text figs. Jena. G. Fischer. 1902.
29. "Über mehrpolige Mitosen als Mittel zur Analyse des Zellkerns." *Verh. d. phys.-med. Ges. Würzburg*, N.F. Vol. 35, pp. 67–90. 1902. Available in English translation, *Foundations of Experimental Embryology*, ed. by Willier and Oppenheimer. Englewood Cliffs, N.J. Prentice-Hall. 1964.
30. "Über den Einfluss der Samenzelle auf die Larvencharaktere der Echiniden." *Arch. f. Entw.-Mech.* Vol. 16, pp. 340–363. Plate XV, 3 text figs. 1903.
31. "Über das Verhalten des Protoplasmas bei monocentrischen Mitosen." *Sitz.-Ber. d. phys.-med. Ges. Würzburg.* 9 pp., 12 text figs. 1903.
32. "Über die Konstitution der chromatischen Kernsubstanz." *Verh. D. Zool. Ges. 13.* Würzburg. 1903.
33. "Noch ein Wort über Seeigelbastarde." *Arch. f. Entw.-Mech.* Vol. 17, pp. 521–525. 1904.
34. *Ergebnisse über die Konstitution der chromatischen Substanz des Zellkerns.* 130 pp., 75 text figs. Jena. G. Fischer. 1904.
35. "Protoplasmadifferenzierung als auslösender Faktor für Kernverschiedenheit." *Sitz.-Ber. d. phys.-med. Ges. Würzburg.* 5 pp. 1904.
36. "Bemerkungen über den Bau der Nierenkanälchen des Amphioxus." *Anat. Anz.* Vol. 25, pp. 599–605. 1 text fig. 1904.

37. "Über die phylogenetische Bedeutung der Sehorgane des Amphioxus." *Zool. Jb.* Suppl. VII: *Festschr. A. Weismann.* Pp. 409–428. 10 text figs. 1904.
38. "Über die Entwicklung dispermer Ascariseier." *Zool. Anz.* Vol. 27, pp. 406–417. 1904. (With N. M. Stevens.)
39. "Über Doppelbefruchtung." *Sitz.-Ber. d. phys.-med. Ges. Würzburg.* 2 pp. 1905.
40. "Zellenstudien V: Über die Abhängigkeit der Kerngrösse und Zellenzahl der Seeigellarven von der Chromosomenzahl der Ausgangszellen." *Jena. Zeitschr. Naturw.* Vol. 39, pp. 445–524. Plates XIX, XX. 1905.
41. "Eine Anfrage an Herrn und Frau Dr. Schreiner in Dröbak." *Anat. Anz.* Vol. 27, pp. 222–223. 1905.
42. *Die Organismen als historische Wesen: Festrede.* 59 pp. Würzburg, H. Stürtz. 1906.
43. "Zellenstudien VI: Die Entwicklung dispermer Seeigeleier. Ein Beitrag zur Befruchtungslehre und zur Theorie des Kernes." *Jena. Zeitschr. Naturw.* Vol. 43, pp. 1–292. Plates I–X, 73 text figs. 1907.
44. "Über Beziehung des Chromatins zur Geschlechtsbestimmung." *Sitz.-Ber. d. phys.-med. Ges. Würzburg.* 10 pp. 1908.
45. "Experimente an Zellkernen." *Berichte d. Senkenberg. naturw. Ges.* Frankfurt a.M. 1908.
46. "Die Blastomerenkerne von Ascaris megalocephala und die Theorie der Chromosomenindividualität." *Arch. f. Zellf.* Vol. 3, pp. 181–268. Plates VII–XI, 9 text figs. 1909.
47. "Über 'Geschlechtschromosomen' bei Nematoden." *Arch. f. Zellf.* Vol. 4, pp. 132–141, 2 text figs. 1909.
48. "Über die Möglichkeit, Ascaris-Eier zur Teilung in zwei gleichwertige Blastomeren zu veranlassen." *Sitz.-Ber. d. phys.-med. Ges. Würzburg.* 5 figs. 1909. (With M. J. Hogue.)
49. "Über die Teilung centrifugierter Eier von Ascaris megalocephala." *Arch. f. Entw.-Mech: Festschr. W. Roux.* Vol. 30, pp. 101–125, 32 text figs. 1910.
50. "Die Potenzen der Ascaris-Blastomeren bei abgeänderter Furchung: Zugleich ein Beitrag zur Frage qualitativ ungleicher Chromosomenteilung." *Festschr. R. Hertwig.* Jena. Vol. III, pp. 133–214. Plates XI–XVI, 24 text figs. 1910.

51. *Anton Dohrn: Gedächtnisrede, gehalten auf dem Internationalen Zoologen-Kongress in Graz am 18. August 1910.* Pp. 1–43. S. Hirzel. 1910. Also in *Verh. VIII Internat. Zool. Kongress zu Graz*, pp. 280–298. 1912.
52. "Über das Verhalten der Geschlechtschromosomen bei Hermaphroditismus: Beobachtungen an Rhabditis nigrovenosa." *Verh. d. phys.-med. Ges Würzburg*, N.F. Vol. 41, pp. 83–97. 19 text figs. 1911.
53. "Über die Charaktere von Echiniden-Bastardlarven bei verschiedenem Mengenverhältnis mütterlicher und väterlicher Substanzen." *Verh. d. phys.-med. Ges. Würzburg*, N.F. Vol. 43, pp. 117–135. 1914.
54. *Zur Frage der Entstehung maligner Tumoren.* 64 pp. Jena, G. Fischer. 1914. Available in English translation by Marcella Boveri, *The Origin of Malignant Tumors, by Theodor Boveri*. Baltimore. The Williams and Wilkins Company. 1929.
55. "Über die Entstehung der Eugsterschen Zwitterbienen." *Arch. f. Entw.-Mech.* Vol. 41, pp. 264–311. Plates VII, VIII, 2 text figs. 1915.
56. "Th. Boveri: Zwei Fehlerquellen bei Merogonieversuchen und die Entwicklungsfähigkeit merogonischer, partiell-merogonischer Seeigelbastarde." *Arch. f. Entw.-Mech.* Vol. 44, pp. 417–471. 1918. Published posthumously by M. Boveri.

OBITUARY PUBLICATIONS

57. *Erinnerungen an Theodor Boveri.* Ed. by W. C. Röntgen. 161 pp. 4 figs. Tübingen. J. C. B. Mohr. 1918.
58. Baltzer, F. "Theodor Boveri." *Naturwissenschaften*, No. 6, 1916.
59. Baltzer, F. *Theodor Boveri: Ein Wegbereiter der Vererbungs- und Zellforschung.* In: *Gestalter unserer Zeit.* Vol. 4. Oldenburg. G. Stalling. 1955.
60. Escherich, K. "Theodor Boveri." *Zeitschr. angew. Entomologie.* Vol. 3, No. 2. 1916.
61. Goldschmidt, R. "Theodor Boveri." *Science*, N.S. Vol. 43. 1916.
62. Hertwig, R. "Theodor Boveri: Ein Nachruf." *Jb. d. K.B. Akad. d. Wiss.* 1916.
63. Hertwig, R. "Theodor Boveri." *Münchener med. Wochenschr.* Nr. 48. 1 portrait. 1915.

64. Korschelt, E. "Theodor Boveri." *Zool. Anz.* Vol. 46. 1916.
65. Nachtsheim, H. "Theodor Boveri." *Naturw. Wochenschr.* Nr. 6. 1916.
66. Spemann, H. "Gedächtnisrede auf Theodor Boveri." *Verh. phys.-med. Ges. Würzburg*, N.F. Vol. 44. 1 portrait. 1916.
67. Spemann, H. "Theodor Boveri." *Arch. f. Entw.-Mech.* Vol. 42.

CITATIONS FROM BOVERI'S
SCIENTIFIC FIELD

Baltzer, F. "Die Chromosomen von Strongylocentrotus lividus und Echinus microtuberculatus." *Arch. f. Zellf.* Vol. 2. 1909.

———. "Zur Kenntnis der Mechanik der Kernteilungsfiguren." *Arch. Entw.-Mech.* Vol. 32. 1911.

———. "Über die experimentelle Erzeugung und Entwicklung von Triton-Bastarden ohne mütterliches Kernmaterial." *Schweiz. naturw. Ges. Neuenburg.* 1920.

———. "Über die Entwicklung von Triton-Bastarden ohne Eikern." *Verh. d. D. Zool. Ges.* 1933.

Beneden, E. van. "Recherches sur la maturation de l'oeuf, la fécondation et la division cellulaire." *Arch. de Biol.* Vol. 4 Ghent. 1883.

Beneden E. van and A. Neyt. "Nouvelles recherches sur la fécondation et la division mitotique chez l'ascaride mégalocéphale." *Bull. Acad. roy. Belg.* 1887.

Boveri, Marcella. "Über Mitosen bei einseitiger Chromosomenbindung." *Jena. Zeitschr. f. Naturw.* Vol. 37. 1903.

Boveri, Margret. *Der Verrat im 20. Jahrhundert.* Pp. 314 ff. Rowohlt. 1960.

Brachet, J. *Biochemical Cytology.* New York. Academic Press. 1957.

Bridges, C. B. "Non-disjunction as proof of the chromosome theory of heredity." *Genetics.* Vol. 1. 1916.

Briggs, R. and T. J. King. "Transplantation of living nuclei from blastula cells into enucleated frog eggs." *Proc. Nat. Acad. Sci. U.S.* Vol. 38. 1952.

———. "Changes in the nuclei of differentiating endoderm cells as revealed by nuclear transplantation." *J. Morph.* Vol. 100. 1957.

Castle, W. E. "The heredity of sex." *Bull. Mus. Comp. Zool. Harvard.* Vol. 40. 1903.

Correns, C. "Gregor Mendels 'Versuche über Pflanzenhybriden' und die Bestätigung ihrer Ergebnisse durch die neuesten Untersuchungen." *Bot. Zeitung.* Vol. 58. 1900.

———. "Über Bastardierungsversuche mit Mirabilis-Sippen." *Ber. D. botan. Ges.* Vol. 20. 1902*a*.

———. "Über den Modus und den Zeitpunkt der Spaltung der Anlagen vom Erbsentypus." *Bot. Zeitung.* Vol. 60. 1902*b*.

Cuénot, L. "La loi de Mendel et l'hérédité de la pigmentation chez les souris." *Arch. Zool. expér. et gén.* (series 3) Vol. 10. 1902.

Delage, Y. "Etudes sur la mérogonie." *Arch. Zool. exp. et gén.* (series 3) Vol. 7. 1899.

Driesch, H. "Entwicklungsmechanische Studien: IV." *Zeit. wiss. Zool.* Vol. 55. 1893*a*.[1]

———. "Entwicklungsmechanische Studien: V, VI." *Zeit. wiss. Zool.* Vol. 55. 1893*b*.

———. "Resultate und Probleme der Entwicklungsphysiologie der Tiere." *Erg. d. Anat. u. Entwges.* Vol. 8. 1898.

———. *Philosophie des Organischen.* Leipzig. Engelmann. 1st ed. 1909; 3rd ed. 1921.

———. *Lebenserinnerungen.* München/Basel. Ernst Reinhardt. 1951.

Dunn, L. C. *Genetics in The 20th Century.* New York. Macmillan. 1951.

Fankhauser, G. "Analyse der physiologischen Polyspermie des Triton-Eies auf Grund von Schnürungsexperimenten." *Arch. Entw.-Mech.* Vol. 105. 1925.

———. "The effects of changes in chromosome number on Amphibian development." *Q. Rev. Biol.* Vol. 20. 1945.

———. "Nucleo-cytoplasmic relations in Amphibian development." *Internat. Rev. Cytol.* Vol. 1. 1952.

Fick, R. "Über die Eireifung bei Amphibien." *Verh. anat. Ges. Tübingen. Anat. Anz.* Suppl. Vol. 16. 1899.

———. "Betrachtungen über die Chromosomen, ihre Individualität, Reduktion und Vererbung." *Arch. f. Anat. u. Physiol. Anat. Abt.* Suppl. 1905.

———. Vererbungsfragen, Reduktions- und Chromosomenhypothesen, Bastardregeln." *Erg. Anat. u. Entw.-Gesch.* Vol. 16. 1907.

———. "Bemerkungen zu Boveri's Aufsatz über die Blastomerenkerne von Ascaris und die Theorie der Chromosomen." *Arch. f. Zellf.* Vol. 3. 1909.

Fleischmann, A. *Die Deszendenztheorie.* Leipzig. A. Georgi. 1901.
Flemming, W. "Beiträge zur Kenntnis der Zelle und ihrer Lebenserscheinungen: II." *Arch. f. mikr. Anat.* Vol. 19. 1880.
———. "Beiträge zur Kenntnis der Zelle und ihrer Lebenserscheinungen: III." *Ibid.* Vol. 20. 1881.
———. *Zellsubstanz, Kern und Zellteilung.* Leipzig. 1882.
Friedrich-Freska, H. "Genetik und biochemische Genetik in den Instituten der Kaiser-Wilhelm-Gesellschaft und der Max-Plank-Gesellschaft." *Naturw.,* Jg. 48. 1961.
Gegenbaur, C. "Die Metamerie des Kopfes und die Wirbeltheorie des Kopfskeletts." *Morph. Jb.* Vol. 13. 1888.
Goldschmidt, R. B. *Erlebnisse und Begegnungen.* P. Parey. 1959.
Goodrich, E. S. "On the structure of the excretory organs of Amphioxus." *Q. J. Micr. Sci.* Vol. 45. 1902; Vol. 54. 1909.
Hadorn, E. "Über die Organentwicklung in bastardmerogonischen Transplantaten bei Triton." *Rev. Suisse Zool.* Vol. 37. 1930.
———. "Die entwicklungsphysiologische Auswirkung der disharmonischen Kern-Plasmakombination beim Bastardmerogon Triton palmatus (♀) × Triton cristatus (♂)." *Arch. Entw.-Mech.* Vol. 136. 1937.
Hartmann, Max. *Gestalter unserer Zeit.* Vol. 4. Oldenburg. G. Stalling. 1955.
Harvey, E. B. *The American Arbacia and other sea urchins.* Princeton Univ. Press. 1956.
Henking, H. "Über Spermatogenese und deren Beziehung zur Eientwicklung bei Pyrrhocoris apterus L." *Zeit. wiss. Zool.* Vol. 51. 1891.
Herbst, C. "Über das Auseinandergehen von Furchungs- und Gewebszellen in kalkfreiem Medium." *Arch. Entw.-Mech.* Vol. 9. 1900.
Hertwig, O. "Beiträge zur Kenntnis der Bildung, Befruchtung und Teilung des tierischen Eies: I." *Morph. Jb.* 1. 1875.
———. "Vergleich der Ei- und Samenbildung bei Nematoden: Eine Grundlage für celluläre Streitfragen." *Arch. f. mikr. Anat.* Vol. 36. 1890.
Hertwig, O. and R. Hertwig. *Über den Befruchtungs- und Teilungsvorgang des tierischen Eies unter dem Einfluss äusserer Agentien.* Jena. 1887.

REFERENCES

Hertwig, R. *Erinnerung an die Feier des 60. Geburtstages von Prof. Dr. Richard Hertwig, 20. Oktober 1910.* Privately printed.
Heuser, E. "Beobachtung über Zellteilung." *Bot. Centralblatt.* 1884.
Hörstadius, S. "Über die Determination des Keimes bei Echinodermen." *Acta Zool.* Vol. 9. 1928.
———. "Studien über heterosperme Seeigelmerogone." *Mém. Mus. roy. d'hist. nat. Belg.* (series 2) No. 3. 1936.
Kühn, A. *Vorlesungen über Entwicklungsphysiologie.* Berlin. Springer. 1955.
Loeb, J. "On the nature of the process of fertilization and the artificial production of normal larvae (plutei) from the unfertilized eggs of the sea urchin." *Amer. J. Physiol.* Vol. 3. 1899.
Mendel, G. *Versuche über Pflanzenhybriden.* Ed. by E. Tschermak. *Ostwalds Klassiker der exakten Naturwissenschaften.* No. 121. Leipzig. 1901.
Morgan, T. H. "A study of variation in cleavage." *Arch. Entw.-Mech.* Vol. 2. 1895.
Morgan, T. H., C. B. Bridges, and A. H. Sturtevant. *The genetics of Drosophila.* The Hague. Nijhoff. 1925.
Naegeli, C. V. *Mechanisch-physiologische Abstammungslehre.* München. 1884.
Pauly, A. *Darwinismus und Lamarckismus: Entwurf einer psychophysischen Teleologie.* 335 pp. München. E. Reinhardt. 1905.
Plate, L. *Die Abstammungslehre.* G. Fischer. 1925.
Rabl, C. "Über Zellteilung." *Morph. Jb.* Vol. 10. 1885.
Rensch, B. *Neuere Probleme der Abstammungslehre.* Stuttgart. Encke. 2nd Ed. 1954.
Roux, W. *Über die Bedeutung der Kernteilungsfiguren.* Leipzig. 1883.
———. "Über die künstliche Hervorbringung halber Embryonen durch Zerstörung einer der beiden ersten Furchungskugeln sowie über die Nachentwicklung (Postgeneration) der fehlenden Körperhälfte." *Virchow's Arch. path. Anat. u. Physiol.* Vol. 114. 1888.
Runnström, J. "Die Analyse der primären Differenzierungsvorgänge im Seeigelkeim." *Verh. D. Zool. Ges.* Tübingen. 1954.
Schleip, W. "Über die Chromatinverhältnisse bei Angiostomum (Rhabdonema) nigrovenosum." *Ber. naturf. Ges. Freiburg i. Br.* Vol. 19. 1911.

Selenka, E. *Die Keimblätter der Echinodermen.* No. 2 of *Studien zur Entwicklungsgeschichte der Thiere.* Wiesbaden. 1883.

Spemann, H., and H. Mangold. "Über Induktion von Embryonalanlagen durch Implantation artfremder Organisatoren." *Arch. Entw.-Mech.* Vol. 132. 1924.

Spemann, H. *Experimentelle Beiträge zu einer Theorie der Entwicklung.* Berlin. Springer. 1936.

———. *Hans Spemann, Forschung und Leben.* Ed. by F. W. Spemann. Verlag Ad. Spemann. 1948.

Strasburger, E. *Neue Untersuchungen über den Befruchtungsvorgang bei Phanerogamen, als Grundlage für eine Theorie der Zeugung.* Jena. 1884.

Strassen, O. zur. "Embryonalentwicklung der Ascaris megalocephala." *Arch. Entw.-Mech.* Vol. 3. 1896.

———. "Über die Riesenbildung bei Ascariseiern." *Arch. Entw.-Mech.* Vol. 7. 1898.

———. "Die Geschichte der T-Riesen." *Zoologica.* No. 40. 1902.

Sutton, W. S. "On the morphology of the chromosome group in Brachystola magna." *Biol. Bull.* Vol. 4. 1902.

———. "The chromosomes in heredity." *Biol. Bull.* Vol. 4. 1903.

Tschermak, E. von. "Über künstliche Kreuzung bei Pisum sativum." *Zeit. landw. Versuchswesen in Österreich.* Vol. 3. 1900.

Ubisch, L. von. "Über Seeigelmerogone." *Pubbl. Staz. Zool. Napoli.* Vol. 25. 1954.

Vries, H. de. "Sur la loi de disjonction des hybrides." *C. R. Acad. Sci. Paris.* Vol. 130. 1900.

Weismann, A. *Die Kontinuität des Keimplasmas.* 1885. (Reproduced in Weismann, A. *Aufsätze über Vererbung.* Jena. G. Fischer. 1892.)

———. *Über die Zahl der Richtungskörper und über ihre Bedeutung für die Vererbung.* Jena. 1887. (Reproduced in Weismann, A. *Aufsätze über Vererbung.* Jena. G. Fischer. 1892.)

———. *Vorträge über Deszendenztheorie.* G. Fischer. 2nd ed. 1904; 3rd ed. 1912.

Weiss, F. E. "Excretory tubules in Amphioxus lanceolatus." *Q. J. Micr. Sci.* Vol. 31. 1890.

Wijhe, J. W. van. "Die Kopfregion der Cranioten beim Amphioxus nebst Bemerkungen über die Wirbeltheorie des Schädels." *Anat. Anz.* Vol. 1. 1889.

Wilson, E. B. "Studies on Chromosomes: I–IV." *J. Exp. Zool.* Vol. 2, 1905; Vol. 3, 1906; Vol. 6, 1909.

———. "The chromosomes in relation to the determination of sex." *Science Progress.* 1910.

———. *The Cell in Development and Heredity.* 1st ed., 1896; 3rd ed. 1925. New York. Macmillan.

PUBLICATIONS FROM THE ZOOLOGICAL INSTITUTE OF WURZBURG 1894–1915

1894. Bömmel, A. von. "Über Cuticularbildung bei einiger Nematoden. Diss. *Arb. zool. zoot. Inst. Würzburg.* Vol. 10.

Knoch, K. "Topographie des Exkretions-Apparates und Nervensystems von Disostomum lanceolatum." Diss.

Lautenbach, R. "Über das Verhalten des Centrosoma bei der Befruchtung." Diss.

Kathariner, L. "Anatomie und Mechanismus der Zunge der Vermilinguier." *Jen. Zeitsch. Naturw.* Vol. 29.

1895. Mayer, O. "Celluläre Untersuchungen an Nematoden-Eiern." Diss. *Jen. Zeitschr. Naturw.* Vol. 29.

Spemann, H. "Zur Entwicklung des Strongylus paradoxus." Diss. *Zool. Jb. Abt. Anat. Ont.* Vol. 8.

1896. Coe, W. R. "Notizen über den Bau des Embryos von Distomum hepaticum." *Zool. Jb. Abt. Anat. Ont.* Vol. 9.

1897. Kathariner, L. "Über Bildung und Ersatz der Giftzähne bei Giftschlangen." *Zool. Jb. Abt. Anat. Ont.* Vol 10.

MacFarland, F. M. "Celluläre Studien an Mollusken-Eiern." Diss. *Zool. Jb. Abt. Anat. Ont.* Vol. 10.

Bott, A. "Über einen durch Knospung sich vermehrender Cysticercus aus dem Maulwurf." Diss. *Zeit. wiss. Zool.* Vol. 63.

1898. Fürst, E. "Über Centrosomen bei Ascaris megalocephala." Diss. *Arch. mikr. Anat.* Vol. 52.

Murray, I. A. "Contributions to a knowledge of the Nebenkern in the spermatogenesis of Pulmonata, Helix and Arion. *Zool. Jb. Abt. Anat. Ont.* Vol. 11.

Spemann, H. "Über die erste Entwicklung der Tuba Eustachii und des Kopfskeletts von Rana temporaria." *Zool. Jb. Abt. Anat. Ont.* Vol. 11.

1899. Wheeler, W. M. "The development of the urinogenital organs of the Lamprey." *Zool. Jb. Abt. Anat. Ont.* Vol. 13.

1901. Schmitt, Fr. "Systematische Darstellung der Doppelembryonen der Salmoniden." *Arch. Entw.-Mech.* Vol. 13.

Bonnevie, K. "Über Chromatindiminution bei Nematoden." *Jen. Zeitschr. Naturw.* Vol. 36.

Spemann, H. "Correlationen in der Entwicklung des Auges." *Verh. Anat. Ges. Bonn.*

———. "Entwicklungsphysiologische Studien am Triton-Ei: I." *Arch. Entw.-Mech.* Vol. 12.

1902. Teichmann, E. "Über Furchung befruchteter Seeigeleier ohne Beteiligung des Spermakerns." Diss. *Jen. Zeitschr. Naturw.* Vol. 37.

Bonnevie, K. "Abnormitäten in der Furchung von Ascaris lumbricoides." *Jen. Zeitschr. Naturw.* Vol. 37.

Spemann, H. "Entwicklungsphysiologische Studien am Triton-Ei: II." *Arch. Entw.-Mech.* Vol. 15.

1903. Leiber, A. "Über Bau und Entwicklung der weiblichen Geschlechtsorgane des Amphioxus lanceolatus" [started by Ludwig Neidert]. Diss. *Zool. Jb. Abt. Anat. Ont.* Vol. 18.

Stevens, N. M. "On the ovogenesis and spermatogenesis of Sagitta bipunctata." *Zool. Jb. Abt. Anat. Ont.* Vol. 18.

Spemann, H. "Über Linsenbildung bei defekter Augenblase." *Anat. Anz.* Vol. 23.

Boveri, M. "Über Mitosen bei einseitiger Chromosomenbindung." *Jen. Zeitschr. Naturw.* Vol. 37.

1904. Zarnik, B. "Segmentale Venen bei Amphioxus und ihr Verhältnis zum Ductus Cuvieri." *Anat. Anz.* Vol. 24.

———. "Über die Geschlechtsorgane von Amphioxus." Diss. *Zool. Jb. Abt. Anat. Ont.* Vol. 21.

Schmidt, H. "Zur Kenntnis der Larvenentwicklung von Echinus microtuberculatus." Diss. *Verh. phys.-med. Ges. Würzburg.* Vol. 36.

Spemann, H. "Über experimentell erzeugte Doppelbildungen mit cyclopischem Defekt." *Zool. Jb.* Suppl. VII: *Festschr. A. Weismann.*

1905. Rubaschkin, W. "Über doppelte und polymorphe Kerne in Tritonblastomeren." *Arch. mikr. Anat. u. Entw.* Vol. 66.

Spemann, H. "Über Linsenbildung nach experimenteller Entfernung der primären Linsenbildungszellen." *Zool. Anz.* Vol. 28.

1907. Leiber, A. "Vergleichende Anatomie der Spechtzunge." *Zoologica*. Vol. 20, No. 51.

Metcalf, M. M. "Studies on Opalina" [preliminary notice]. *Zool. Anz.* Vol. 32.

———. "The excretory-organs of Opalina." Part 2. *Arch. Protistenk.* Vol. 10.

Spemann, H. "Neue Tatsachen zum Linsenproblem." *Zool. Anz.* Vol. 31.

1908. Hoffmann, R. "Über Fortpflanzungserscheinungen von Monocystideen des Lumbricus agricola." Diss. *Arch. Protistenk.* Vol. 13.

Baehr, W. B. von. "Über die Bildung der Sexualzellen bei Aphididae." *Zool. Anz.* Vol. 33.

Baltzer, F. "Über mehrpolige Mitosen bei Seeigeleiern." Diss. *Verh. phys.-med. Ges. Würzburg.* Vol. 39.

Heffner, B. "Über experimentell erzeugte Mehrfachbildungen des Skeletts bei Echiniden-Larven." Diss. *Arch. Entw.-Mech.* Vol. 26.

Artom, C. "Über ein Verfahren, die beschalten Eier von Ascaris megalocephala mit jedem gewünschten Konservierungsmittel zu fixieren." *Zeitschr. f. wiss. Mikr. u. mikr. Technik.* Vol. 25.

1909. Baltzer, F. "Über die Entwicklung der Echinidenbastarde mit besonderer Berücksichtigung der Chromatinverhältnisse." *Zool. Anz.* Vol. 35.

———. "Die Chromosomen von Strongylocentrotus lividus und Echinus microtuberculatus." *Arch. f. Zellf.* Vol. 2.

Baehr, W. B. von. "Die Oogenese bei einigen viviparen Aphididen und die Spermatogenese von Aphis saliceti mit besonderer Berücksichtigung der Chromatinverhältnisse." *Arch. f. Zellf.* Vol. 3.

Boring, A. M. "A small chromosome in Ascaris megalocephala." *Arch. f. Zellf.* Vol. 4.

Dingler, M. "Über die Spermatogenese des Dicrocoelium lanceatum Stil. et Hass. (Distomum lanceolatum)." Diss. *Arch. f. Zellf.* Vol. 4.

Boring, A. M. "On the effect of different temperatures on the size of the nuclei in the embryo of Ascaris megalocephala, with remarks on the size-relation of the nuclei in univalens and bivalens." *Arch. Entw-Mech.* Vol. 28.

Stevens, N. M. "The effect of ultra-violet light upon the developing eggs of Ascaris megalocephala." *Arch. Entw.-Mech.* Vol. 27.

1910. Zarnik, B. "Vergleichende Studien über den Bau der Niere von Echidna und der Reptilienniere." *Jen. Zeitschr. Naturw.* Vol. 46.

Baltzer, F. "Über die Beziehung zwischen dem Chromatin und der Entwicklung und Vererbungsrichtung bei Echinodermenbastarden." *Arch. f. Zellf.* Vol. 5.

Hogue, M. J. "Über die Wirkung der Centrifugalkraft auf die Eier von Ascaris megalocephala." Diss. *Arch. Entw.-Mech.* Vol. 29.

1911. Kautzsch, G. "Über Auftreten und Teilungen abnorm grosser zweiter Richtungskörper." *Verh. D. zool. Ges.* 1911.

Baltzer, F. "Zur Kenntnis der Mechanik der Kernteilungsfiguren." *Arch. Entw.-Mech.* Vol. 32.

Gulick, A. "Über die Geschlechtschromosomen bei einigen Nematoden nebst Bemerkungen über die Bedeutung dieser Chromosomen." Diss. *Arch. f. Zellf.* Vol. 6.

Edwards, Ch. L. "The sex chromosomes in Ascaris felis." *Arch. f. Zellf.* Vol. 7.

1912. Kautzsch, G. "Studien über Entwicklungsanomalien bei Ascaris: I." *Arch. f. Zellf.* Vol. 8.

1913. Ubisch, L. von. "Die Anlage und Ausbildung des Skelettsystems einiger Echiniden und die Symmetrieverhältnisse von Larve und Imago." Diss. *Zeitschr. f. wiss. Zool.* Vol. 104.

———. "Die Entwicklung von Strongylocentrotus lividus." *Zeit. wiss. Zool.* Vol. 106.

———. "Über das larvale Muskelsystem von Arbacia pustulosa." *Verh. phys.-med. Ges. Würzburg*, N. F. Vol. 42.

Kautzsch, G. "Studien über Entwicklungsanomalien bei Ascaris: II." *Arch. Entw.-Mech.* Vol. 35.

Baltzer, F. "Über die Chromosomen der Tachea (Helix) hortensis, Tachea austriaca und der sogen. einseitigen Bastarden T. hortensis × T. austriaca." *Arch. f. Zellf.* Vol. 11.

———. "Die Herkunft der Idiochromosomen bei Seeigeln." *Sitz.-Ber. d. phys.-med. Ges. Würzburg.*

Oehniger, M. "Über Kerngrössen bei Bienen." *Verh. phys.-med. Ges. Würzburg.* Vol. 42.

Vonwiller, P. "Über den Bau der Amöben." Diss. *Arch. f. Protistenk.* Vol. 28.

1915. Mehling, E. "Über die gynandromorphen Bienen des Eugster-

schen Stockes." Diss. *Verh. d. phys.-med. Ges. Würzburg.* Vol. 43.
Geinitz, B. "Über Abweichungen bei der Eireifung von Ascaris." Diss. *Arch. f. Zellf.* Vol. 13.
Ubisch, L. von. "Über den Einfluss von Gleichgewichtsstörungen auf die Regenerationsgeschwindigkeit." *Arch. f. Entw.-Mech.* Vol. 41.

Glossary

ANIMAL, VEGETATIVE. Terms for the two primary poles of the egg; the animal pole, where the polar bodies originate, marks a region tending to be rich in protoplasm, whereas the vegetative region contains relatively more yolk (fig. 15*a*).

BLASTOMERES. The cells into which the egg is subdivided during cleavage (fig. 12*b-e*).

BLASTULA. Early, spherical, one-layered embryonic stage, which precedes the formation of the primitive digestive cavity (fig. 12*f*).

CHROMOSOMES. Elongated or rounded bodies composed of the chromatin of the nucleus; the principal carriers of the hereditary factors (fig. 1*c* and *d*).

CYTOPLASM. The cell protoplasm external to the nucleus.

DARWIN, CHARLES, 1809-1882. English naturalist who founded modern evolutionary theory.

DEVELOPMENTAL PHYSIOLOGY. Study of the causal mechanisms of embryonic development.

DIFFERENTIATION. The development of different cell types from the originally similar cells of the blastula (fig. 12*g* and *h*).

DIPLOID. Cells with a double chromosome set, derived equally from the maternal and paternal germ cells. Haploid cells contain a single set, corresponding to only one of the germ cells.

EVOLUTION. Process of transformation of species and larger categories of plants and animals; theory of phylogenetic origin of modern organisms.

FRANCONIA. The northern part of what is now Bavaria.

GAMETES. Reproductive cells: egg and sperm (fig. 4).

GASTRULA. Primitive two-layered embryonic stage in animal development, which follows the blastula. A simple "archenteron," or primitive digestive cavity, is present (fig. 12h).

GENE. Hereditary factor in the chromosome; the unit of Mendelian heredity.

GONAD. The reproductive gland, ovary or testis.

Gymnasium. In German-speaking countries, the gymnasium is a high school for students about 15–19 years of age, finishing with the *Maturität* which admits a student to the university. The *gymnasium* includes approximately the first two years of an American college.

Habilitation. A doctor of philosophy may be promoted to *Privatdozent* on presenting a *Habilitationsschrift*, a scholarly contribution of higher quality than the doctoral thesis.

HAPLOID. *See* diploid.

KARYOKINESIS. Nuclear division that involves doubling of the chromosomes and their distribution to the daughter cells (fig. 1).

LAMARCK, J. B., 1744–1829. French zoologist who originated one of the early evolution theories. According to him, characteristics acquired by one generation could be inherited by succeeding ones.

MACROMOLECULE. Molecule of very large size such as those of proteins or nucleic acids.

MATURATION (of germ cells). Processes by which the primordial germ cells in the gonads become functional sperm or eggs. In both sexes this involves a reduction of the chromosome set to the single or haploid condition by "maturation divisions" (fig. 11); in the case of the egg, polar bodies are extruded in the process.

MEROGONY. Development of an embryo from an egg fragment.

MITOSIS. *See* karyokinesis.

PARTHENOGENESIS. Development of the egg in the absence of fertilization by sperm.

PHYLOGENY. The history or evolution of major groups (phyla, classes) of animals or plants.

PHYLUM. The largest classificatory grouping of organisms, characterized by common body plan (for example, Chordata, Arthropoda).

PLASMA. *See* protoplasm.

PLUTEUS. Early larval stage of the sea-urchin (fig. 12i).

GLOSSARY

POLAR BODY. Tiny abortive cell given off at the animal pole of the egg as a result of a maturation division.

POTENCY. All developmental possibilities present in an embryo or portion thereof under both normal and experimental conditions.

PREFORMATION THEORY. The theory that the embryo develops from preformed parts of the egg, in mosaic fashion.

Privatdozent. Lowest ranking lecturer in a German university.

PROTOPLASM. Active "living" substance of the cell; in Boveri's day this term was frequently used as synonymous with *cytoplasm*.

ZYGOTE. A fertilized egg cell.

Index

Adaptation, 131, 136–141
Amphioxus, 13, 126; nephridia in, 38, 126–127; photoreceptors in, 128–129, 137, 138
Ascaris, 10; chromosomes of, 63, 65–67; discovery of, 63; double fertilization in, 119, 122–123; as experimental material, 63, 106, 120–121; fertilization in, 72, 74, 75; germ-line and somatic development in, 115–117; maturation in, 63–64; mitosis in, 63, 65, 73; tetrasters in, 74, 89, 122–123. *See also* Chromosome
Aster, 61; astral rays, 73; in dividing cells, 74. See also *Ascaris*; Sea urchin

Baltzer, Fritz, 27–36 *passim*, 84, 88
Bamberg, 4, 6, 11, 12, 18, 41, 42, 45, 47
Beneden E. van: on *Ascaris* fertilization, 72–73; and chromosome continuity, 65; and discovery of *Ascaris*, 63–65; and distribution of chromosomes, 62; and identical chromosome division, 119; and "idioplasm," 63
Blastomere: definition of, 159; development of, in sea urchin, 89, 90–91, 109–112; of frog, 107; separation of, 55
Boveri, Marcella, 16, 17, 18, 90
Boveri, Margret, 18, 22
Boveri, Victoire, 11, 12, 15, 44, 45
Boveri, Walter, 11, 12, 44, 49

Bridges, C. B., 101
Briggs, R., 84
Bütschli, Otto, 129

Cancer, 103–105
Cell, 60; differentiation, 118–119, 124–126, 159; germ and somatic cells in *Ascaris*, 115–125. *See also* Cytoplasm; Mitosis; Nucleus
Centrosome: in cell division, 73–75; centrosome theory of fertilization, 60, 64, 88; centrosphere, 74, 88; in dispermy, 88; origin of, 73
Chromosome: of *Ascaris*, 10, 63–67, 89; as carrier of different gene groups, 98–102; continuity of, 64–65; definition of, 159; distribution of, in dispermic sea urchin egg, 88–94; DNA in, 69; doubling of, 62; *Drosophila* salivary chromosome, 101, 102, 126; "idioplasm," 62–63; nucleoplasmic ratio and nuclear size, 78; as organized structures, 66–69, 102; relation to malignant tumors, 103–105; role in development, 83, 85–97; of *Sagitta*, of salamander, 65; sex chromosome, 96
Chromosome diminution, 114–125
Correns, C., 98
Cytoplasm: concentration gradient in, 113, 121; definition of, 159; effect of centrifugation on, 124; polarity in,

163

110–112; role in chromosome diminution, 119, 121–122, 124; role in development, 78–85, 90, 105–126

Darwin, C., 131, 135–136, 159
Delage, Y., 82
Deoxyribonucleic acid. *See* Nucleic acid
Differentiation. *See* Cell
Diminution. *See* Chromosome diminution
Dispermy. *See* *Ascaris*; Mitosis; Sea urchin
Dohrn, A., 10, 39, 40–41, 50
Driesch, H.: and experiments on totipotency of sea urchin cells, 106, 107, 109–110; on mortality in double-fertilized sea urchin eggs, 55; scientific character of, 113–114; on tetrafoil cleavage, 88, 91
Drosophila, 24, 68, 94, 101–102, 126

Evolution: Boveri's views on, 130–142; definition of, 159; of multicellular forms, 133–134

Fankhauser, G., 84
Fertilization: Boveri's theory of, 69–75; centrosome theory of, 64; double fertilization in *Ascaris*, 122–123; double fertilization in sea urchin eggs, 85–99; of sea urchin eggs, 73; of sea urchin egg fragments, 76–85; studies in *Ascaris*, 63. *See also* O. Hertwig
Fick, R., 66–68
Fleishmann, A., 131
Flemming, W., 62
Formative centers. *See* Centrosome

Gastrula, 107, 160
Gegenbaur, C., 127, 129
Gene, 98–99, 160
Germ line, 115–117, 123
Goldschmidt, R., 21, 95
Goodrich, E. S., 127

Hadorn, E., 84
Haider, K., 43, 47, 48
Haploid sea urchin, 76–85
Henking, H., 96
Herbst, C., 20, 55, 90, 110
Hermaphroditism, 96, 97

Hertwig, O., 20; and chromosome individuality theory, 63, 66; and experiments with sea urchin fragments, 76–78; on fertilization, 71–73; and use of sea urchin, 69–70
Hertwig, R.: Boveri's association with, 7, 8, 10, 13, 14; and experiments with sea urchin egg fragments, 76–78; influence of, 30, 36, 63
Hesse, R., 38, 128
Heuser, E., 65
Hörstadius, S., 84, 112
Hybridization. *See* Sea urchin

Karyokinesis, 160. *See* Mitosis
King, T. J., 84
Kölliker, R. A. von, 63
Kupffer, C. von, 7, 117

Lamarck, J. B., 130, 131, 140–142, 160
Leuckart, R., 115
Linkage, 102
Loeb, J., 75, 78, 84

Maturation, 63–64, 160
Mendelian heredity, 97–101
Merogonic hybridization. *See* Sea urchin
Metschnikoff, E., 115
Miescher, F., 103
Micromeres, 107
Mitosis: definition of, 160; multipolar (dispermy), 74–75; normal, 62, 74, 88; in tumors, 104–105; unipolar, 17
Morgan, T. H., 24, 89, 91, 101
Munich, 6–14 *passim*, 28, 30, 36

Naples, 10, 28, 29, 31, 39, 40, 41, 43, 50–56 *passim*, 90
Naegeli, C. V., 62, 63
Nephridia. *See* *Amphioxus*
Notochord, 126
Nucleic acids, 69, 102, 103
Nucleoplasmic ratio and nuclear size.
Nucleus: as carrier of heredity, 76–85; division of, 62, 63, 73–74; haploid, 81, 82; nuclear transplantation, 84; size of, 78. *See also* Chromosome; Cytoplasm; Mitosis

Paracentrotus. *See* Sea urchin
Parthenogenesis, 75, 78, 97, 160

INDEX

Pauly, A., 8–10, 18, 36, 43, 48, 130–131, 141, 142
Photoreceptors. See *Amphioxus*
Phylogeny, 131, 133–140, 160
Pluteus. *See* Sea urchin
Polar bodies, 63, 161
Polyembryony, 139
Preadaptation, 139
Psammechinus. *See* Sea urchin

Rabl, C., 65, 66
Rhabditis nigrovenosa. *See* Threadworm
Röntgen, W. C., 40, 49
Roux, W., 86, 107, 124

Sagitta. *See* Chromosome
Salamander, 65
Schleip, W., 97
Sea urchin: chromosome number of, 92; development and potency of blastomeres and their parts, 55, 88, 89, 107, 109–112; development of haploids, 76; dispermic studies in, 55, 56, 85–99; eggs and sperms as experimental material, 70; eggs' visible polarity, 55, 106, 110–112; fertilization in, 70–71; merogonic hybridization, 76–85; nuclear transplantation, 84; *Paracentrotus*, 55, 79–85, 110–112; pluteus (larva), 76–85, 94, 160; *Psammechinus*, 79–85; *Sphaerechinus*, 79–85; structure, cleavage, and development of eggs, 106–107
Selection, 131, 132

Solenocytes, 127
Spemann, H., 19, 20, 21, 22, 23, 27, 28, 33, 35, 36–39, 126, 135, 141
Sphaerechinus. *See* Sea urchin
Spindle, 62, 73, 74. *See also* Mitosis
Strasburger, E., 63, 119
Strassen, O. zur, 38, 119, 121, 123–124
Sutton, W. S., 98–99

Threadworm, 96–97
Tschermak, E. von, 98

Ubisch, L. von, 84–85

Villefranche, 55
Vries, H. de, 98

Weismann, A., 24; and chromosome as carrier of hereditary material, 85–86; on chromosome diminution, 119, 121–124; on evolution, 130, 131, 133, 136, 138; and primordial germ cells, 115; and theory of chromosome combination, 53, 63; and theory of germplasm, 117; and unequal division of chromosomes, 119
Weiss, F. E., 127
Wien, W., 23, 24, 34–37, 49, 92
Wijhe, J. W. van, 127–128
Wilson, E. B., 13, 23, 28, 58, 69, 75, 95, 105, 106, 115, 125
Würzburg, 14–17, 19, 21, 22, 25, 41, 42, 44, 46, 48, 129, 130; Zoological Institute in, 27–41, 141

www.ingramcontent.com/pod-product-compliance
Lightning Source LLC
Chambersburg PA
CBHW021709230426
43668CB00008B/774